Awakening
to
Kabbalah

Awakening to Kabbalah

The Guiding Light of Spiritual Fulfillment

Rav Michael Laitman, PhD

Awakening to Kabbalah:
The Guiding Light of Spiritual Fulfillment

2006 First Printing
© 2006 by Michael Laitman

For information regarding permission to reprint material from this book, please mail or fax your request in writing to Jewish Lights Publishing, Permissions Department, at the address / fax number listed below, or e-mail your request to info@kabbalahbooks.info.

CONTENTS

Preface

Out of all known creatures, the human being is the most complete. Yet it is the human who asks the eternal question, repeated in every generation: "What is the purpose of creation?"

Scientists have been trying to find the reason for our existence for centuries, and yet they have failed to find the answer. The question grows more and more acute with each passing generation, because the pains of the world only increase in time, and the struggle for survival continues. Hence, it is quite possible that the answer is not within our reach, and science simply cannot provide it.

But the question is not just "Why do things exist?" but also "What am I living for?" The evolutionary processes of nature and living organisms astonish us with their inconceivable contradictions. For example, young animals mature in a matter of weeks or months, while humans need many years to grow. Only at the end of the process do you see that humans are the masters of creation; however, during the transitional phases, humans are much weaker than any other animal. If we did not know the final outcome, we would reach the opposite conclusion—that it is the young animal who will become the master of creation and the human who will lead a bitter life and die. It follows that we understand neither the meaning of our existence, nor the reason behind the evolutionary process.

We perceive the world through our five senses. What we perceive by sight, sound, smell, taste, and touch then unite to form our image of the world around us. Therefore, if we had other senses we would feel the world differently. It is common knowledge that dogs "see" the world through their sense of smell, and to the bees the world appears to be divided into billions of cells.

If we can perceive only a small portion of all that exists around us, and in a very limited range, is it then possible to *feel* everything around us? Can it be that this is where the secret to the purpose of our existence lies? If this is so, then we need another sense, a sixth sense, to discover what we cannot feel with the other five senses. How can we acquire that sense? Why are we not given that sense at birth?

There is a simple answer to these questions. It is up to us to develop this sixth sense. Because humans are very different in their development from all other creatures, they acquire or develop everything with a human, moral effort. And once we have acquired this additional sense, we differentiate ourselves from the beast once and for all. Out of all living creatures, we humans are the only ones with the ability to discover in ourselves that hidden sense and develop it.

Humankind evolves gradually, from generation to generation. We evolve technologically, scientifically, culturally, but not ethically. At a certain point in their evolution, people must feel an inner need for spiritual development, a need to discover that extra, hidden sense, or else they will not endure. Kabbalah is the method for the discovery of that sense.

The evolution of humanity is like the evolution of the individual: It evolves through infancy, childhood, adolescence, and adulthood. During this process, it uses every means at its disposal. Then, when we discover that extra sense within, we begin to feel a wider world around, to see the meaning of life, the reason for suffering, and the purpose of existence. Those feelings enable us to control the world, to uproot the source of pain and head toward the goal of discovering the meaning of life.

The purpose of this book is to help those of you who are interested in spirituality. Many sources, and most notably the Zohar, have pointed to our moment in history as the age of Kabbalah. Our souls have evolved over many centuries, through many difficult periods in history, and we now possess the spiritual readiness and desire to go beyond our limited physical existence and rise above this transitory world. The large-scale movements and popularization of Kabbalah through workshops and meditation retreats are merely small signs that our time has come. We are now able to start developing the sixth sense, and by so doing, we will change ourselves and, by extension, the world around us for the better.

ACKNOWLEDGMENTS

Many, many people contributed to the making of this book. They have given their precious time and outstanding abilities; I am in debt to all.

My first thanks are to Marc Daniels and his wife, Adrienne E. Hacker Daniels, PhD, whose initial initiative and zeal are the very reasons you are reading these lines.

I would like to thank Benzion Giertz for the original compilation and supervision of the Hebrew version. I would also like to thank Chaim Ratz for his sensitive and intelligent translation.

I would like to thank the entire Jewish Lights Publishing staff, but the hard work and dedication of some is worth special notice: Alys R. Yablon, Jewish Lights Publishing Jerusalem-based editor, for her sensitive and thoughtful editorial assistance without which this book would not have been so accessible to the reader; Emily Wichland, vice president and managing editor of Jewish Lights, who was so helpful in managing the development of the book from its conception to its final word; and Lauren Seidman, project editor, who carefully brought the draft into its completed form.

Last but by no means least, I would like to express my deepest and most sincere gratitude to Stuart M. Matlins, founder and publisher of Jewish Lights, whose wise assistance and personal care were crucial to the successful completion of this book. I have already published over thirty books, in many countries and with many publishers, but it was especially pleasurable for me to work hand in hand with this master of making books. His advice and counseling I will always treasure.

INTRODUCTION

Every authentic Kabbalah book contains terms that depict suffering, such as beating, affliction, and torment. As in the Bible, Kabbalah uses these terms to refer to any state of being that is less than ideal. The Creator's purpose in creation is to do good to His creations. Thus, if a desire to take pleasure in something is not realized immediately, it is defined as suffering. It is written in the Gomorrah that if you put your hand in your pocket expecting to pull out three coins and find that there are only two, you are already suffering.

The wisdom of Kabbalah speaks of receiving eternal, unlimited pleasure in every desire that surfaces or that will surface in every person. It speaks of a life where happiness is acquired effortlessly. Nature (which is *Elohim*—God—in Gematria) urges us to obtain that perfect state. Therefore, every state that is *less* than that is considered suffering.

Kabbalists, who receive unending pleasure and feel their existence as eternal, beyond life and death, where there is only gain and no loss, measure all situations compared to their own state of being. They say all of us *must* reach that state sooner or later. In order to accelerate our development to the ultimate good, they often describe our state as incidental, temporal life, infested with torment (such as injustice, hunger, poverty, greed, jealousy, and selfishness). Because we are used to our present condition, we do not feel our lives as they depict them. We do not see any other way to exist, and see that everyone is struggling for survival. For that reason it is hard for us to understand the statements of Kabbalists and evaluate our lives through their eyes.

Nevertheless, it would be unwise to discard their depictions offhand, because at the end of the day, their intention is to impel us toward the best state of existence possible. In many ways, they are like parents motivating their children to reach the best, most pleasurable state. Their books are recommendations, tips that help us all correct and direct our hearts, and consequently our lives, toward success, tranquility, peace, and above all—happiness.

KABBALISTS ABOUT THE WISDOM OF KABBALAH

WHO SHOULD STUDY KABBALAH?

On the learning of the Zohar there are no restrictions.

—The Hafetz Chaim (1843–1933)

If my generation had listened to my voice, they would have started to study the book of Zohar at the age of nine.

—Rabbi Isaac from Kamarna, *Notzer Chesed* (1806–1874)

One who feels within, after several attempts, that one's soul within is in peace only when engaging in the secrets of Torah, one should know for certain that this is what one has been made for. Let no preventions—corporeal or spiritual—stop one from running to the source of one's life and true wholeness.

—Rabbi Abraham Yitzhak HaCohen Kook,
Orot Kodesh 1, 88–89 (1865–1935)

The Torah was given to learn and to teach so that all will
know the Lord, from least to greatest. We also find many
books of Kabbalists alerting of the importance of the study of
the wisdom that everyone must learn.

—Rabbi Yitzhak Ben Tzvi Ashkenazi,
The Purity of Sanctity, 147 (d. 1807)

May it be that the holy flock would begin their study of the
holy Book of Zohar when they are still small, nine and ten
years old ... and redemption would certainly come without any
Messiah labor-pains.

Rabbi Shem Tov had already written in The Book of Faith
that Judea and Israel will be salvaged for ever only through
the wisdom of Kabbalah, because this is the only Godly
wisdom given to the sages of Israel from days and years of
old and through it the glory of God and His Holy Torah
shall be revealed.

—Rabbi Shabtai Ben Yaakov Yitzhak Lifshitz, *Segulat Israel*
(The Remedy of Israel), system 7, item 5 (1845–1910)

Let not the neuter say, "For I am a dry tree, and who am I to
approach inside the holy into the books of Kabbalah?" The
righteous have already agreed that this is the inclination's
counsel and a lie today. Even when not understanding every-
thing, the words of the Holy Zohar are still able for the soul
and good for every soul of Israel; small and great are there,
each according to the root of his soul.

—Rabbi Tzvi Hirsh Ben Yaakov Horovitz, *Hanhagot Yesharot*
(Upright Guidance), item 5 (d. 1873)

My brother, being troubled with business, either in wealth or
d forbid) in great poverty, does not rid you (God forbid) of
ing in this wisdom, for whatever are you living for, and
d all this been revealed to us? Why had the Creator

revealed in our generation what He did not reveal except in the generation of Rabbi Akiva and Rabbi Shimon Ben Yochay and his friends, the study of the wisdom of the Ari? You are not rid of the internality of the Torah, for without it man is like a hay-eating beast, as it is written in the Tikkunim of the verse "All flesh is grass."

—Rabbi Tzvi Hirsh Eichenstein of Ziditchov,
Keep from Evil, 29 (1763–1831)

Indeed, if we set our hearts to answer but one very famous question, I am certain that all these questions and doubts will vanish from the horizon, and you will look unto their place to find them gone. This indignant question is a question that the whole world asks, namely, "What is the meaning of my life?" In other words, these numbered years of our life that cost us so heavily and the numerous pains and torments that we suffer for them, to complete them to the fullest, who is it that enjoys them? Even more precisely, to whom do I give delight?

It is indeed true that historians have grown weary contemplating it and particularly in our generation. No one even wishes to consider it. Yet the question stands as bitterly and as vehemently as ever. Sometimes it meets us uninvitingly, pecks at our mind and humiliates us to the ground before we find the famous ploy to flow mindlessly in the currents of life as yesterday.

—Rabbi Yehuda Leib HaLevi Ashlag (Baal HaSulam),
Introduction to the Study of the Ten Sefirot, item 2 (1884–1954)

WHY DISSEMINATE THE WISDOM?

Do have strength my soul-mate to shine the light of the wisdom of the hidden in the world. The time has come now for every one to know that the salvation of Israel and the entire world depends but on the appearance of the wisdom of the

*hidden light of the Torah in a clear tone. And the hidden will
also raise the revealed to its feet.*

—Rabbi Abraham Yitzhak HaCohen Kook, *Igrot 2* (1865–1935)

*I have seen it written that the prohibition from above to
refrain from open study in the wisdom of truth, was only for a
limited period, until the end of 1490, but from then on the
prohibition has been lifted and permission was granted to
study The Zohar. Since 1540 it has been a great Mitzvah
(very good deed) for the masses to study in public,
old and young ... and that is because the Messiah will
come because of that and not because of any other reason.
Therefore, we must not be negligent.*

—Rabbi Chaim David Yosef Azulai (The Chidah),
Introduction to Ohr HaChama, 81 (1724–1806)

Redemption depends primarily on the study of the Kabbalah.

—The Vilna Gaon, *Even Shlema* 11,13 (1720–1797)

*Only through the expansion of the wisdom of Kabbalah in the
masses will we obtain complete redemption.... Both the individual and the nation will not complete the aim for which they
were created, except by attaining the inner part of the Torah
and its secrets.... Hence, it is the great expansion of the wisdom within the nation that we need first, to merit receiving the
benefit from our Messiah. Consequently, the expansion of the
wisdom and the coming of our Messiah are interdependent.
Therefore, we must establish seminaries and compose books,
to hasten the circulation of the wisdom throughout the nation.*

—Rabbi Yehuda Leib HaLevi Ashlag (Baal HaSulam),
Introduction to the Tree of Life, item 5 (1884–1954)

*When enlightenment diminishes from the Children of Israel in
the course of the exile, and the Godly precedence vanishes and*

forgotten from them, many will fall in the pits of corporeality.... This will be because the secrets of the Torah will vanish from them. Not many will be wise and know the secret, only one in a city, and many will swim in the ditch of error.

—Rabbi Moshe Kordoviro (The Ramak), *Know Thou the God of Thy Father*, 139–40 (1522–1570)

And will know the secrets of the Torah and the taste of the Mitzvot ... because the soul is strengthened by them and is isolated with its Maker.... And besides the good that is hidden in the next world for the delving and learning in it, in this world too they taste the taste of the next world. By the virtue of the delving, the Messiah will come, for then the earth shall be full of knowledge, and this will be the reason to hasten His coming.

—Rabbi Isaiah Ben Abraham HaLevi Horowitz (The Holy Shlah), *First Article*, 30 (1565–1630)

I have news about the city of Prague ... and how Judaism is declining there day-by-day.... Indeed, it is that previously the revealed Torah was sufficient; but now in the days of the Messiah, there must be the teaching of the hidden too.... Before, the evil inclination was not as strong, and the revealed Torah was sufficient as a cure for it. But now, before the redemption, the evil inclination is increasing, and we must be strengthened with the hidden too.

—Rabbi Simha Bonim of Pshisha, *The Torah of Joy*, 57 (1767–1827)

We must know it, for we are commanded to it: "Know this day, and lay it to thy heart, that the Lord, He is God." Thus, we are committed to know and not only to believe, but rather with matters that reason with the heart.

—Rabbi Moshe Chaim Lutzato (The Ramchal), *The Book of the War of Moses*, Rules, 349 (1707–1746)

THE BENEFITS

*The attainment begins from the hidden Torah, and only after-
wards does one attain the remaining portions of the Torah,
and only in the end does one attain the revealed Torah.*

—The Vilna Gaon, *The Siddur* (1720–1797)

*This revelation will not be, but through the study of the Torah.
But the redemption depends primarily on the study of the
Kabbalah.*

—The Vilna Gaon (1720–1797)

*In the future, only with the help of the book of Zohar will the
children of Israel go out from the exile.*

—Rabbi Shimon Bar Yochay, *Parashat Nasoh*, Book of Zohar
(c. 2nd Century CE)

*While the orthodoxy continues to insist solely on Gomorrah
and Mishnah, rejecting the Agada, the Kabbalah and the
research … it impoverishes itself, and all the means that it
applies to defend itself, without adopting the real potion of
life, i.e. the internal light of the Torah, will not help. It will be
filled with anger … for the obvious and tangible that is apparent in Torah and Mitzvot alone, can never, under any circumstances bring one to one's goal, in any generation, and all the
more so in ours. It is possible only alongside the expansion of
the many spiritual roots.*

—Rabbi Abraham Yitzhak HaCohen Kook,
Igrot 2 (1865–1935)

*Upon studying this composition, one awakens the power of the
souls and those righteous people, along with the force of
Moses … for when they practice it, they renew the renewed
Light that was renewed upon writing this composition, and*

divinity shines and illuminates from that Light as it did when it was (innovated,) and all who study it, reawaken the benefit and that former Light that Rabbi Shimon Bar Yochay and his associates had uncovered upon making the composition.

—Rabbi Moshe Kordoviro (Ramak), *Ohr Yakar,* gate 1, item 5 (1522–1570)

The Study of the book of Zohar is preferable and above all other studies.

—Rabbi Chaim David Yosef Azulai (The Chidah) (1724–1806)

Woe unto them who make the spirit of Messiah vanish from the world, so as never to return, make the Torah dry, without the moistness of mind and knowledge, for they confine themselves to the practical part of the Torah, and do not wish to try to understand the wisdom of the Kabbalah, to know and educate themselves in the secrets and the reason behind the Torah and the Mitzvot (commandments). Alas, they cause by their deeds the poverty, the ruin and the robbery, the looting, the killings and destruction in the world.

—*Tikkunei Zohar,* Tikkun 30

The study of the corrections of The Holy Zohar ... purifies the body and the soul, and has the virtue of bringing redemption soon in our days.

—Matte Efraim

Even when one does not have the vessels, when one engages in this wisdom, mentioning the names of the Lights and the vessels related to one's soul, they immediately shine upon us to a certain measure. However, they shine for him without clothing the interior of his soul for lack of the able vessels to receive them. Despite that, the illumination one receives time after time during the engagement draws upon one grace from above,

imparting one with abundance of sanctity and purity, which
bring one much closer to reaching perfection.

—Rabbi Yehuda Leib HaLevi Ashlag (Baal HaSulam), *Introduction*
to the Study of the Ten Sefirot, item 155 (1884–1954)

When one as much as reads the words ... what is it like? It is
like a sick person who drinks a therapeutic potion that helps
although one is not proficient in the wisdom of medicine.

—Rabbi Moshe Zechuta (Remez), part 3, 2 (1625–1698)

All the great Kabbalists cry out unanimously, that as long as
they remove the secrets from the Torah and do not practice its
secrets, they destroy the world.

—Rabbi Abraham Yitzhak HaCohen Kook, *Igrot* 2 (1865–1935)

ISRAEL AND THE NATIONS

The revival of the nation is the foundation for the construction
of the great repentance—the repentance of Israel and the
repentance of the world, which will follow.

—Whisper to Me the Secret of God, from the
Sayings of Rav Kook

Israel—a nation that complete universalism is rooted deep
within its soul.

—Whisper to Me the Secret of God, from the
Sayings of Rav Kook

But if, ... one of Israel degrades the virtue of the internality of
the Torah and its secrets, ... as though it were, God forbid,
redundant, by that one causes degradation and decline of the
internality of the world, which are the Children of Israel, and

*intensifies the domination of the externality of the world—
meaning the Nations of the World—over them. They will
humiliate and disgrace the Children of Israel, and regard
Israel as superfluous, as though the world has no need for
them, God forbid.*

—Rabbi Yehuda Leib HaLevi Ashlag (Baal HaSulam),
Introduction to the Book of Zohar, item 69 (1884–1954)

*Rabbi Elazar Bar Abina says, "No calamity comes to the
world, but for Israel."*

—*Talmud Bavli,* Masechet Yevamot, 63

1

GREAT KABBALISTS THROUGHOUT HISTORY

Because of our ability to absorb various pictures and impressions of the world around us, we can describe what we feel in this lifetime and create books from our experiences. But Kabbalah books describe what a person who experiences both the physical world and the upper, spiritual world at the same time feels, something that others do not perceive.

Such is the uniqueness of the books of Kabbalah. They describe things an ordinary person cannot feel, though they are attainable. A Kabbalist is not just a person who feels the upper world, but someone who can describe emotions in a clear language so that anyone can understand them. Thus, by studying these books, we will be able to nurture the missing senses inside us, the ones with which we will be able to feel the upper world to the point where we can see our past and future lives. After all, "there is no time in spirituality." Through Kabbalah, we can all attain the sensation of the eternal upper world and live willingly in both worlds at once.

There is a special force in books of Kabbalah: any person who studies them under the right guidance can attain the spiritual degree of the author. That is why it is crucial that we know which books to study. There are many books of Kabbalah, written in various styles and forms and written by Kabbalists at various degrees of attainment. We now know which of the books are the ones that help us enter the spiritual world and which of them direct us like a guidebook intended for a person lost in a foreign country.

There are several ways to describe the spiritual worlds. The spiritual world and our own world are parallel. Everything in the spiritual world comes down to ours. All the events originate in the upper world. They descend from it to ours and clothe the suitable objects of this world very accurately.

Nevertheless, we should refrain from thinking that there is spirituality within our material world. Spirituality stands as an abstract force behind this world's objects and manages the entire process unfolding in this world. This stems from the verse in the Torah, "Thou shalt not make unto thee a graven image, nor any manner of likeness," being a prohibition to see anything that has to do with godliness and spirituality in corporeal things.

There is not an object, phenomenon, or force in this world that is not a consequence of the upper world. Therefore, Kabbalists use words taken from our world to describe spiritual objects, for they are the roots of all our world.

An ordinary person, as yet without a spiritual screen, relates to books of Kabbalah as if they were fairy tale stories of things that happen in our world. But Kabbalists will not be confused by the words, for they know precisely from which branch they stem and which consequence in our world correlates to the root in the spiritual world.

That is how the Torah was written. The books of the prophets, however, were written in a different language, the language of legends, whereas the Talmud describes the laws of the spiritual world as acts, laws, and commandments that exist in our world. Thus, even behind the words of the Talmud we should see the objects and actions of the upper world.

In the following sections, we will outline the major books of Kabbalah from the beginning of time until today, and their authors, the great Kabbalists throughout history.

ADAM, THE FIRST MAN

The history of Kabbalah corresponds to the history of humankind. It begins at the same time Adam appeared on earth, who (as tradition has it) was the first man. With Adam begins the spiritual evolution of humankind. Adam was the recipient of the first Kabbalah book: *The Angel Raziel (Hamalaach Raziel)*.

A person who lives in this world feels the nature of the world within him or her, as well as the nature of the world around. People who feel both worlds simultaneously are called Kabbalists. The first man sensed those two worlds and described them in his book. That book is now available to us, containing interesting drawings with explanations and diagrams that the first man wrote by himself.

When one opens the book, it is evident that the author is not an uncivilized, uneducated mammoth hunter. He was a Kabbalist of a very high degree. He discovered the fundamental secrets of creation. He studied the upper world, the world where our souls roam before we are born and descend to this world and where they return after our physical death.

The first man, who was also the first soul that came down to our world, tells us about the evolution and descent of the rest of the souls. He does not tell us about the bodies that would be born in our world, but about those souls that come out of his own, the souls of his children, grandchildren, and great-grand-children. He tells us about the entire humanity that would stem from him, what will happen to it, and when it will rise once more to the root from which it came.

He tells us how these souls will regroup into one soul, a soul that exists on a much higher level than our own, of which we are but fragments. That is what he tells us in *The Angel Raziel*. The word *raziel* comes from the Hebrew word *raz*—the angel of secrets who reveals the secrets of creation.

ABRAHAM THE PATRIARCH

The primary book that came into our possession after the book of the first man was the book of Abraham the Patriarch, *The Book of Creation (Sefer Yetzira)*. It is a special book and a difficult one to understand, because it is very synoptic, containing only several dozen pages. We've known about its existence for thousands of years, but it is impossible to study Kabbalah with it because Abraham did not mean to introduce a study book for those in our world and explain how to develop the sensation of the upper spiritual world. His purpose was not to teach the attainment of the upper world, but only to mark out a few principal laws that he discovered about that world.

However, Abraham the Patriarch described the various interconnections between our world and the spiritual world and demonstrated how the spiritual world operates, where the spiritual forces come from, and how they clothe the bodies of this world. The book explains how each body receives a special force from above, which determines what will happen to it in our world and what will finally become of it—that is, what humanity will attain under the influence of the upper forces.

The Book of Creation was written in a different way than *The Angel Raziel*. It is comprised of chapters (called *mishniot*), and its language is better organized. Abraham writes about the structure of the spiritual world, about the ten *sefirot* (properties of the spiritual reality), *partzufim* (spiritual objects, or systems), and management systems, how the upper force (the light) descends, how it is balanced and collected, and how the collective soul is divided into individual souls that descend in a certain order. He writes about relationships between the bodies in this world, under the influence of the souls that clothed them. Although the book is interesting, it is very far removed from today's souls and can only serve as a learning aid because of its great power.

The property that characterizes Abraham is called *hesed* (benevolence). Abraham was known for his hospitality. His book gives humanity his power of *hesed,* which allowed the following generation to develop and aspire toward spiritual attainment. But the generation that followed Abraham demanded a new revelation, which resulted in the emergence of new Kabbalists.

MOSES, THE TORAH, AND THE LANGUAGE OF THE BRANCHES

The next significant composition, after *The Book of Creation* and *The Angel Raziel,* is the book of Zohar, but between Abraham the Patriarch and the Zohar there were many great Kabbalists, the greatest of whom was Moses.

Moses was known for being different than other Kabbalists in that alongside the revelation that he obtained, he was ordered to make it known to the whole of humankind. That did not happen with previous Kabbalists. Since then, all Kabbalists form study groups.

Moses had seventy disciples, and Yehoshua Ben Nun (Joshua, the son of Nun) was the one who ultimately inherited both his wisdom and leadership. Moses did more than research the upper world. He dealt with the practical realization of his spiritual attainment in our world, such as the exodus from Egypt. With the wisdom he acquired and the upper forces he

received from above, he was able to bring the people of Israel
out of exile.

Moses's task was to deliver the people of Israel out of
Egypt and write a book with which any man could "conquer"
the upper world and leave Egypt in the spirit—stop worshiping
idols, objects, the sun, and other false gods. He wanted to
enable people to obtain entry into the spiritual land of Israel,
called the world of *Atzilut*—a world of eternity and wholeness.
It is a situation that one attains inwardly, beyond the boundaries of time and space.

The method Moses introduced in his book is called Torah,
from the word *ohr* (light). It contains instructions on how to
use the light to enter the spiritual world, how to live for an eternal goal instead of the transient life we live in this world. With
this book, a person can uncover the entire picture of creation,
though he or she may experience just a tiny fraction of it. He or
she can calculate correctly and attain the desired outcome,
build his or her life toward the final goal, the one Moses
wanted to attain. That is what a person who studies the method
that Moses developed gradually achieves.

Moses's method, resulting from the Torah, allows anyone
living on earth to attain his spiritual level, meaning that he or
she can exit this world with his or her feelings and enter the
upper world, the entire creation. The Hebrew root of the name
Moses is the word *moshe,* which means pulling out of this
world. The Torah is a historic tale about the exodus of the people of Israel from Egypt. But in fact, it depicts an exit from a
state of corporeal lowness called Egypt to a higher state called
"The Land of Israel."

Moses used the language of the branches. He used names
of objects, feelings, and actions of our world, but intended to
point to objects in the spiritual world: supreme powers, secret
forces, exits and entries of power, and information and effects,

including harmful ones. All of these themes are portrayed as a historic tale about human development. In fact, the Torah describes a certain era in human development, but it actually refers to spiritual roots.

If we do not interpret the Torah solely as a historical document, we are then able to perceive spiritual forces that come from the upper world to ours. Instead of flesh and blood figures, such as Moses and Pharaoh, or animals and nations, we will see spiritual forces. If we remove the outer shell from the Torah, we will see an entirely different picture, detached from this world. Then, gradually, we will come into contact with these forces and use them for spiritual elevation.

With the help of his seventy disciples, Moses composed a guide to spiritual ascent. He made several copies of it and taught it in groups that together became known as the "people of Israel." Thus, the people of Israel originated from a group of Kabbalists, the disciples of Moses, and belonging to that nation is determined by a striving for spirituality. Hence, anyone from the nations of the world who feels a desire for spirituality can become a Jew.

The Jews are that group of people who adopted the concept of monotheism in the time of Abraham. After Abraham's death, a group of people who believed in a single force of leadership, a force one could turn to, was established. The successors of Abraham, who called themselves Jews, were unique in that they wanted unity with the Creator, *dvekut* (adhesion) with Him. They were also called Hebrews from the Hebrew word *ivri*, meaning one who crossed over from this world to the spiritual.

In the book of Torah, Moses developed a science for attaining contact with the upper world. But for most people, it is difficult, if not impossible, to see anything deeper than family sagas and history. We will not even be able to feel what is concealed in it, as Kabbalists tell us.

USING THE ZOHAR TO READ THE TORAH

People search for all kinds of codes in the Torah and find all the possible interconnections among its parts. Indeed, the parts of the Torah are interconnected in an infinite number of ways—the number of the letters, the words, the verses, and the phrases have been calculated. Recently, a fantastic work of calculation analyzed the inner structure of the letters and parts of letters. But those calculations give us nothing. They don't teach us what stands behind each symbol or dot, or the shape of the letters and their combinations.

The Torah was first written as a single word with no spaces. Only later was that single word divided into individual words and the words into letters, and those letters were further broken down to their parts. In the end, these parts become a point and a line that extends from it. A black point on a white background symbolizes the source of the light: the light emanates from the single point. If the light descends from the upper force, from the Creator to the creature, it is a vertical line; if the force is ascribed to the entire creation, it is a horizontal line.

This is all the information that we get from the Creator. All the possible combinations between dots and lines depend on those two signs sent to us from the Creator:

- The vertical line—a personal sign sent to humankind by the Creator

- The horizontal line—a general sign sent to humankind by the Creator

- All the situations in between

All the signs combined created the code for the relationship between God and humankind, and at any moment things can appear different because at any moment the soul is in a different state.

A person who looks at the letters of the Torah, provided he or she has learned to read it correctly, can see his or her own past, present, and future through the combinations of dots and lines. But to see these things, one needs a key. With it, one can read the Torah like a tour guide to the spiritual world as opposed to simply a historic episode. This key is found in the Zohar, which interprets the Pentateuch and explains exactly what Moses meant by writing the Torah.

When we study the five books of the Pentateuch through the eyes of the Zohar, we see something entirely other than our world; we see the upper world, the spiritual leadership of our world, and the entire creation. That is why Kabbalists read those two books together.

Before printing the book of Zohar, Moses's students and followers wrote, over several hundred years, basic interpretations of incidents in the Torah so that we could better understand what Moses had written. The first interpretation of the Torah is the Mishnah, from the word *sheni, shanah* (something that repeats itself). The Mishnah portrays all the spiritual laws as laws of this world. It explains what one must and must not do. We know these explanations as Mitzvot (commandments, precepts) of "do" (positive precepts) or Mitzvot of "do not do" (negative precepts).

Only Kabbalah can explain these actions. It explains that the most important thing is not the worldly act, but the aim in the spiritual world. What a person does with his or her internal intentions matters. That is precisely what the sages and the disciples of Moses tell us about.

The Talmud was the next generation, whose sages explained the right way to keep the Mitzvot in each and every situation. But they also understood that it was not about the mechanical observation of Mitzvot in our world, but rather that through these Mitzvot, in their correct spiritual context, we may study the nature of our world and the upper world in the best way for us.

Though the Mishnah and the Talmud explain each spiritual law in detail, they are written in everyday language. Hence, if you do not have the code for the book of Zohar, you only see the Mishnah and the Talmud as recommendations for the right way to lead a religious, orthodox way of life.

All great Kabbalists, meaning all those sages of the Mishnah (the *Tanna'im*) and the Talmud (the *Amora'im*), explained in their texts the system of creation and how we can best use its laws. They explained the reason why these forces come down to us and how we can use them to get a positive response and ultimately become vital and active parts of creation.

When these forces come to us from above and we react to them correctly, our responses climb up again and bring down to our world good results for everyone. This is the task of Kabbalah, also called the wisdom of Kabbalah. The word *Kabbalah* comes from the word *lekabel* (to receive), meaning to learn how to receive the abundance that comes to us from the upper forces correctly.

A person who begins to study Kabbalah can clearly see that the reason for all the pains and catastrophes we experience both on the personal and global level is that we do not correctly interpret what happens around us. Because of our benighted behavior and incorrect reaction, our situation and the consequences that return to us increasingly worsen.

Kabbalah is the most practical science. It provides humanity the key to the leadership of the world. But for us to lead it, we must first study it. For that we need to know the general structure of the universe and its system of management, so that we may know how to take an active part in it.

RABBI SHIMON BAR-YOCHAI
(SECOND CENTURY CE)

Rabbi Shimon Bar-Yochai (Rashbi) was the author of the book of Zohar, which was written in the second century CE. It is the most important work of Kabbalah and considered to be its primary and most fundamental textbook. Rashbi lived between the Talmudic period and that of the Zohar and is regarded as a great researcher of both human nature and the upper world. He is also among the most important sages of the Talmud (his name is mentioned there some four thousand times). He was proficient in the languages of both the Talmud and Kabbalah, and he used both of them to describe the upper system of management, how the events of the present and the future are made to happen there—all the innovations and transformations—and how they come down from there to our world and manifest themselves in the clothing of this world.

The Zohar explains which actions influence the rest of the world from here below. Rashbi was the first Kabbalist to describe the reactions that we get from above for our thoughts. He described how they operate in the upper world and thus affect the unfolding of future events that are to descend to us. The Zohar is crucial to us because it encircles all the possible circumstances throughout human history.

Before Rashbi began to write the Zohar, he established around him a group of disciples, where the soul of each disciple corresponded to a certain spiritual degree in the upper world. There were nine students, and he was the tenth. Together they formed one collective soul, corresponding to the complete structure in the spiritual world called the *Eser* (ten) *Sefirot*.

Thus, although Rashbi is the author of the book, each and every one of the students represents one of the attributes of the spiritual world he describes. He built a sort of prism, through which the simple upper light descends to our world and divides into ten parts, which are then divided into ten inner *Sefirot*. Their story is in fact a description of how those ten spiritual properties or forces come upon our world and lead it and how each person can use these forces for his or her own benefit and for others.

Rashbi said he could not have written the book by himself. He was supposed to write the book for the last generations and, in the meantime, conceal it so that it would only be revealed in the sixteenth century. To write this book in such a way that the intermediary generations would pass it by, he used his disciple Rabbi Abba. Rabbi Abba began writing the book while hearing and studying it from his teacher, but he wrote it in such a way that those who read it perceive only the outermost layer of the book.

The more people work on themselves, the further they refine themselves and rise spiritually. As they rise, they become better qualified to delve into the depth of the Zohar and actually feel what is written in it. They receive spiritual forces and become increasingly able to take an active part in the overall evolution.

Rabbi Abba did not write the Zohar in Hebrew, as Abraham and Moses wrote their books. Instead, he wrote it in Aramaic, which was a language used in Mesopotamia (today's Iraq). The book also contains words in Greek and Latin that were prevalent at the time. However, that does not diminish the value of the book in any way. In writing this way, the author wanted to hide the book's inner meaning, wrapping it in an unappealing package.

To write the Zohar, Rabbi Shimon Bar-Yochai hid in a cave in the northern part of Israel (the Idra Raba) with his son Rabbi Eleazar. They sat in a cave for thirteen years, eating—as the Midrash has it—carobs and drinking water from a nearby spring. Their clothes were torn, so to stay covered, they buried themselves in sand. During the day, while buried, they studied and examined everything, and later wrote what they learned in the book of Zohar.

When the thirteen years had passed, Rabbi Shimon left the cave with his son and gathered ten disciples around him. He raised them spiritually, each according to his individual soul, thus building a collective spiritual vessel in which they felt the structure of the upper world, the highest root of our existence.

When the book was finally written, Rabbi Shimon passed away and was buried in Miron, not far from where the book was written. His son is buried next to him, and his other disciples are also buried nearby.

The Zohar was concealed while Rabbi Shimon was still alive, right after the writing was completed. Humanity as a whole, and especially the Jewish people, were not at the spiritual degree that would have allowed them to use the book for a spiritual purpose and for the good of all humankind.

The Torah also speaks only of spiritual worlds, but it has spread so well throughout the world precisely because it was written so that everyone can understand it at his or her corporeal level and adhere to what it says. Moses referred to spiritual laws, but he did it so that those who adhered to those laws would direct the entire illumination of the universe on him- or herself in the best possible way. Because of the coded and "simple" way the Torah was written ("simple" because when we read it, we *think* that it is simple and clear), the Torah didn't have to be concealed like the Zohar, and could remain out in the open and not handed over secretly from one Kabbalist to another.

Rabbi Shimon ordered the Zohar buried in his lifetime. In fact, he both wrote it and concealed it. Today, many parts of the Zohar are still missing. Five or six hundred years later, the book was found by chance: a Kabbalist asked one of his students to get some food from the market. The student returned with food wrapped in paper. The Kabbalist was astonished to see that the wrapping was an ancient manuscript.

The Kabbalist began to study it and saw that it led to the secrets of creation. He immediately sent his students back to the market. They burrowed in every pile of trash and gathered all the pages they could find, eventually ending up with more than 2,700 pieces of paper. An Arab merchant, who had come to Israel after a camel ride in the area of the rivers of Euphrates and Tigris, had found these pieces of paper along the way and thought to use them as wrappings for his spices. Thus the pages of the ancient book of Zohar were put together again.

The Kabbalist Moshe De Leon was the first to publish the Zohar in thirteenth-century Spain. It contained not only commentaries on the Torah, but commentaries on other books as well, such as the books of the prophets and Kabbalistic explanations to the Mishnah and the Talmud. Therefore, what we now refer to as the Zohar is only a part of the original book. It is not a large book today, containing approximately three hundred pages of text, and is about twenty times smaller than the original size, meaning that a huge amount of information is still missing. However, this is not so great a loss, because new Kabbalists have come along and told us about everything that happens in the two worlds and how the upper world affects our own, building today and tomorrow. Except for the interpretation of Moses's five books of the Pentateuch, almost nothing else remained. However, even in its present form, it remains a key by which we can open the gates to the spiritual world.

After Rabbi Moshe De Leon, the Zohar was concealed again for hundreds of years, until the late Middle Ages, the time of the Holy Ari.

THE ARI (1534–1572)

In each generation, the same souls that existed in previous generations reappear. They are clothed in new bodies, evolve, and become more sensitive and receptive to sublime and complex spiritual knowledge. Thus, people who lived thousands of years ago had the same souls as our own but are more developed today, bringing technological and spiritual progress to our world.

Any progress in humankind is the result of souls rising to a higher degree, after having gained experience in previous lives. Each soul that comes to our world begins its life with the experiences it has accumulated in the previous life. Hence, the soul goes through a process of accumulating knowledge, spiritual attainments, and worldly sensations, leaving it with memories we call *reshimot* (reminiscence).

Of all the souls that have come down to our world from previous generations, only a few have wished to evolve into the spiritual realms. However, in our time, many have done so. We are much more advanced than our ancestors. It is easier for us to absorb new information and live it, because we are born prepared to absorb this information. Hence, each new piece of data is completely natural for us.

Kabbalah books tend to be revealed and concealed intermittently. They can be hidden for several generations, reappear, and then be lost again. It happens this way so that humanity can go through certain "corrections" *(tikkunim)*. Generally speaking, these books exist throughout the history of humankind to correct humanity and assure its development. All these books will be known to everyone in the future. The Zohar and the books of the prophets state that in our final days, all humanity will use these books as manuals for attaining the upper worlds, and people will have happy, eternal, and complete lives.

Souls of great Kabbalists go through special cycles. They do not appear in our world in every generation but, like the books, only in special ones. The soul of the first man incarnated later on in Abraham the Patriarch, Moses, Rabbi Shimon Bar-Yochai, the Holy Ari, and, in our days, Rabbi Yehuda Ashlag.

Such a soul comes only during special times, when it is meant to influence and correct the entire human race.

In the sixteenth century, the time of the Middle Ages and barbarism, a child was born in Jerusalem. Later in his life he received the name the Holy Ari. He absorbed the entire Kabbalistic knowledge since the first man and processed it and phrased it in such a way that all the generations following him could receive their spiritual nourishment from his books.

The Ari later moved to Egypt. His father passed away while the Ari was young, and he went to live with his uncle. At thirty-five he came to Tzfat, an ancient city in Israel that at the time of the Ari was home to many Kabbalists.

The Ari taught in a school he had arranged for his disciples for eighteen months and then died at age thirty-six. His first disciple was Chaim Vital, who was twenty-eight at the time. Chaim Vital wrote down everything he'd heard during those eighteen months, and what he wrote comprised the twenty volumes we know as the writings of the Ari. When the Ari passed away, he left his work to Chaim Vital and no one else. Chaim Vital was the only one permitted to practice Kabbalah after the demise of the Ari and publish the writings of his teacher.

What distinguishes the Ari is not only that his soul was an incarnation of the souls of giant Kabbalists, but also that it was born precisely at the time when the general level of souls in the world demanded spiritual evolution. The first phase of the evolution of the souls ended with the Ari—a phase of unconscious evolution, the Middle Ages, a time of barbarism and savagery.

The appearance of the Ari brought with it a new era of human development. Souls that awaken a desire for spirituality and knowledge of the upper world began to descend and clothe themselves in the bodies of our world. This caused the end of the Middle Ages and the beginning of the Renaissance. It was a time of evolution, leading to the industrial revolution.

The Ari was given permission from above to renew the system that existed back in the days of the first man and change it from a system for unique, individual souls to one that is suitable for the masses—a large number of souls who evolved previously in this world and were now ready for spiritual ascent.

The Ari received the book of Zohar in the sixteenth century. He taught his students all the Kabbalistic sources that preceded him. Later on, these sources were published in one book, called *The Tree of Life (Etz Hayim)*. It is a textbook that teaches about the way to the spiritual world, explaining how we can rise and attain perfection and eternity.

The Ari wrote some twenty other books in addition to *The Tree of Life*. They are very difficult to understand, but today they form the basis for the entire method of Kabbalah. In those books, the Ari describes the laws of creation as a clear scientific system, in a way that could be used in textbooks for study. The primary part of the Ari's books is divided into eight parts called "Eight Gates." Each gate describes a certain topic in Kabbalah in a clear, scientific manner. He explains the laws of the upper world, how humans influence these laws, and the reincarnations.

All the books of the Ari were written in a new and completely different approach, suitable for the souls beginning the correction of the world. Many Kabbalists all over the world relied on his work, especially in Eastern Europe, Ukraine, White Russia, and Poland. Many were drawn to Kabbalah, and a mass movement called Hasidism was established on the basis of it. The Hasidim are people who are drawn to connect with the upper spiritual world. They see that there is a sublime goal to their worldly lives.

Studying the books of the Ari raises us beyond the level of our world. The Ari stated that anyone who felt a desire for the spiritual world could study his books. Before the Ari, the special soul of a Kabbalist would descend as if by grace from above, and the right book for that generation would appear. But since the time of the Ari, anyone with any kind of desire for spirituality can study Kabbalah, and by learning from his books, one can enter the upper world. We have already stated that in every generation the same souls return, clothed in new bodies and retaining their previous experiences. Therefore, each generation is wiser than the last and aspires for something higher.

During the time of the Ari, the general evolution of the souls was such that souls desired spiritual elevation and were not satisfied with a mere ordinary life on the level of this world. That desire was the beginning of the Renaissance and the industrial revolution. In spirituality, this process is expressed by the desire to discover the origin of life, to search for the answer to the question: "What is the meaning of my life?" From the time of the Ari onward, that question began to ripen in the souls that descended. It made people search for the origin of life. This search takes us to the study of the upper world from which we come, though we cannot actually feel and understand it. The Ari took the wisdom of Kabbalah and created an entirely new system, suited for souls that want to rise by themselves.

Before the Ari, two types of souls came to this world: one, the beastly kind, was concerned only with procreation and preservation of the species, while the other, the Kabbalistic souls, were independently occupied with studying the spiritual world. Since the time of the Ari, the souls that descend to our world can no longer settle for the beastly sustenance of this world. They have evolved to such a degree that a great many of them want to rise to the spiritual world.

Today, souls are acquiring desires for independent spiritual ascent, and they need a method to help them come to the spiritual world. The Ari was the first to establish such a method and thus is considered the most important Kabbalist. The Ari writes that since the establishment of his method, any person wishing to study Kabbalah can do so, regardless of his age, sex, or nationality.

After the Ari, many people began to open up to Kabbalah. Hundreds of souls began to rise independently and break through to the spiritual world. The last phase of human development begins with the Ari. Starting in the sixteenth century, souls embarked on a new spiritual birth, attaining complete entrance to the spiritual world while still clothed in their corporeal bodies. This prosperous time continued until approximately the 1920s. Without the method of the Ari, the spiritual world would have been inaccessible to such a large number of souls. The prosperity was especially noticeable in Eastern Europe, where many Kabbalists emerged, establishing many movements in Judaism.

At the time of his early death, some of the Ari's texts were buried with him, some were hidden in a box by his relatives, and Chaim Vital himself began to work on others. Gradually, the books were written and printed. Shmuel Vital, Chaim Vital's son, carried on the work of his father, and his son, Chaim Vital's grandson, continued after him, publishing the books of the Ari. The Ari's grave was opened some three generations after his demise and the rest of his scriptures were dug out. They were composed into the Eight Gates, the primary texts of the Ari.

Thus we see that even the followers of the Ari were not in possession of all his compositions. Even Chaim Vital did not have sufficient knowledge to compose a comprehensive and concise method, suitable for every soul that descends to this world, despite the tremendous efforts he made to preserve those texts for us.

RABBI YEHUDA ASHLAG, BAAL HASULAM
(1884–1954)

In the end, neither the Zohar nor the writings of the Ari were intended for a systematic study of the Kabbalah. Although the Kabbalah is indeed a science, before the twentieth century there never was a true textbook. It is only in our days that a comprehensive and concise method suitable for all souls of this world was established. To fill in the gaps, Rabbi Yehuda Ashlag, the great Kabbalist who was born in Warsaw in 1884 and lived in Jerusalem from 1922 until his death in 1954, wrote a commentary on the Zohar and the texts of the Ari. Rabbi Ashlag, called Baal HaSulam (Master of the Ladder), evolved while writing the commentaries and published his principal work, *The Study of the Ten Sefirot (Talmud Eser Sefirot)*, considered the predominant Kabbalah study book of our time.

This textbook consists of six volumes, containing more than two thousand pages. It includes everything that Kabbalists have written since the dawn of time: the writings of the first man, Abraham the Patriarch, Moses, Rabbi Shimon Bar-Yochai, and the Holy Ari. This book displays Kabbalah in a concise manner, fit for study. Thus, we have with us today everything needed to learn how creation was made, how it comes down to us, and how we can influence it from below, all the way to the highest world, to have the future we'd like to have.

Today the Zohar is incomprehensible without the Sulam commentary. Yet, the method of Baal HaSulam is often misunderstood. To those who have not achieved spiritual fulfillment, the book may be perceived as dry, schematic, and unemotional. It can read like an instruction manual rather than something that moves our heart. But this perception stems from a lack of understanding.

Studying Kabbalah means attaining what the books speak of, not just knowing what is written in the books. Unlike any other science, with Kabbalah you become the subject of the research as you study, so the things about which you read happen inside of you rather than on the page.

Some say that all we must do is read, which then triggers something in the world above, which we do not understand. But this contradicts the desired outcome of the study, the purpose of the study, and what we should be doing. One should rise to the spiritual world while living in this world, in this corporeal life. That, in fact, is the purpose of the system of Kabbalah, and it can only be achieved through the right study, with the real books, written by Rashbi (Rabbi Shimon Bar-Yochai), the Ari, and Baal HaSulam.

When we learn from *The Study of the Ten Sefirot* under the right conditions and with the proper guidance, the upper world opens. There is a special approach to the material in the book and a special key that explains how to read the text, to make it open correctly. When a person studies like that, he or she begins to feel the universe, to see and feel in every sense what exists beyond the range of that sense, because his or her senses are corporeal and limited and can perceive nothing beyond their scope.

Baal HaSulam writes in the introduction to the *Study of the Ten Sefirot* that anyone can attain the highest point of spiritual evolution in our world, anyone can attain equivalence of form with the upper force—the Creator. We can attain the highest spiritual state while living in this world, because the body no longer stands as a barrier between the upper world and the soul. It doesn't matter if the soul is clothed in a body or not, because we can freely move from world to world and exist in all the worlds simultaneously in a state of eternity and perfection. Then, we become timeless, motionless, and spaceless.

Baal HaSulam writes that using his method makes all these phases attainable and that his method is suitable for everyone without exception. Besides the *Study of the Ten Sefirot*, Rabbi Ashlag also wrote a commentary on the Zohar and on the writings of the Ari. Baal HaSulam writes that he is a reincarnation of a soul that starts with the first man, continues through Abraham the Patriarch, Moses, Rabbi Shimon Bar-Yochai, the Ari, and finally him. Because of that, he could take the compositions of these Kabbalists and process and present them to us in a way that suits our generation.

Although Baal HaSulam lived in our generation, much the same thing happened to his writings as happened to the Zohar and the writings of the Ari: some of his writings were concealed and are only now being published. I myself have many manuscripts of Baal HaSulam in my possession that my students and I are preparing for publication. These manuscripts are a spiritual inheritance I received from my rabbi, Baruch Ashlag, the son of Baal HaSulam.

RABBI BARUCH ASHLAG, RABASH (1907–1991)

Baruch Ashlag represents the next phase in the evolution of Kabbalah after his father. The eldest son of Yehuda Ashlag, Baruch Ashlag was born in Poland in 1907 and came with his father to Israel at age fifteen. He always worked simple jobs: he was a construction worker, a road builder, a shoemaker, and a clerk. Never ashamed to do any work, he knew that jobs are necessary to survive in this world and nothing more. He was offered quite a few high offices, but never accepted any of them.

Although he was very knowledgeable in Torah and Talmud, Baruch Ashlag never served as a community rabbi. Instead, he spent his entire life following in the footsteps of his father and advancing in the study of Kabbalah. When his father passed away, Baruch Ashlag inherited his disciples and continued his work. He published the Zohar with his father's commentaries, as well as several other books.

I myself came to him in 1979, having already been in search of a teacher for four years. I was studying by myself and with all kinds of "Kabbalists." I went a long way knowing I needed to study Kabbalah, but not knowing who could teach me. From the first lesson with Rabbi Ashlag, I knew he was the right instructor for me. I remained with him for twelve years, until his death. When he died, I was there at his bedside.

Rabbi Baruch Ashlag wrote five books of articles, called *Shlavey Hasulam* (The Rungs of the Ladder), in which he successfully expressed all the inner states of a person who is on the way toward attaining the upper world. He studied all the possible phases, every step and movement that a person makes on the way, and explained how to reach the spiritual world and how to feel and live in it.

He constructed a system by which the individual could attain the upper world, something that previous Kabbalists did not do. This unique aspect of his articles is especially significant for those who want to attain the spiritual world. Without those articles, it is impossible to even imagine getting beyond our physical reality.

He also left us a manuscript of sermons he had heard from his father, which he called *Shamati* (I heard). Using these articles, we can define the characteristics of our own spiritual state and learn how to continue the spiritual ascent in that specific situation. The book is the basis for all the phases in the spiritual worlds and their many combinations, which affect the soul of one who aspires to attain them.

The works of Rabbi Baruch Ashlag are essential to us and to anyone who wishes to be open to the spiritual world. After the death of Rabbi Ashlag, a group was established, called Bnei Baruch (The Sons of Baruch). Together, we continue to study in the way he paved.

2

In the Beginning

The book of Genesis begins:

> In the beginning God created the heaven and the earth. Now the earth was unformed and void, and darkness was upon the face of the deep; and the spirit of God hovered over the face of the waters. And God said: "Let there be light." And there was light. And God saw the light, that it was good; and God divided the light from the darkness. And God called the light Day, and the darkness He called Night. And there was evening and there was morning, one day (Gen. 1:1–5).

Every one of us, when hearing these verses, is moved in some way. Over the years we have been exposed to various interpretations of the verses of the Torah on the literal level. However, we rarely settle for the simplified interpretations that leave many questions open. We want to analyze the Torah scientifically, logically. What does the Torah really talk about? And most importantly, what for?

All the holy Scriptures speak of one thing only—the upper world and how it was created and how the upper world created our world. The Bible doesn't just describe what one finds in that world, but also teaches one how to see it. The gradual revelation of the upper world is called the "spiritual ascent," or the degrees of spiritual rise. The wisdom of Kabbalah is a science that teaches the structure of the upper world, using sophisticated language, drawings, and schemes. The Torah describes the upper world for us in an ordinary language.

If we try to translate the language of the Torah into the language of the Wisdom of Kabbalah, we see that the Torah describes for us the process of the creation of the upper world, its structure, the design of its development, and after that it depicts the process of humankind's creation. However, the Torah does not refer to a person of our corporeal world. Rather it refers to the creation of the will to receive, called "soul" or "man" *(Adam)*, and to the purpose of fulfilling this will to receive, this creation, with total, eternal, and complete pleasure. The desire for pleasure is actually the only creation. Besides that there is only the Creator. Thus, everything besides the Creator is no more than various degrees of the will to receive pleasure. That is also the situation in our world: the difference between all creatures and objects is only in the different levels of their will to receive pleasure, and that is what determines the properties of each and every creature.

The desire to receive is divided to five sublevels, marked as:

1. The tip of the letter *yod* (ʼ), which correlates to the *Sefira* of *Keter*

2. The letter *yod* (ʼ), which correlates to the *Sefira* of *Hochma*

3. The letter *hey* (ה), which correlates to the *Sefira* of *Bina*

4. The letter *vav* (ו), which correlates to the *Sefira* of *Tifferet*

5. The letter *hey* (ה), which correlates to the *Sefira* of *Malchut*

Together these letters form the word *Yod* (י), *Hey* (ה), *Vav* (ו), *Hey* (ה). This is also the name of the Creator, because creation feels the Creator, and the letters express the four basic manifestations of the Creator in creation. The five parts of the desire are called *sefirot,* and their names are *Keter, Hochma, Bina, Tifferet,* and *Malchut.*

In Kabbalah, gender is determined according to function. The active is for the most part considered a male and the passive, a female. For that reason, the Creator is considered a male (as we will refer to Him throughout this book) and creation, a female.

The Creator wishes to fill creation with pleasure "to the brim," to the full sensation of perfection and eternity. That means that what the Creator wishes to give us is His own state of being. He is perfect and unique and because of that perfection He wants to give His state of being, meaning His perfection, to creation. Hence, the purpose of creation is the attainment of the perfection of the Creator and the ability to receive what He wants to bestow.

The seven days of creation referred to in Genesis are felt by humanity as seven thousand years. The first six stand for the six days of the week, during which humanity corrects itself unconsciously at first and finally consciously, through great efforts. In the end, we will reach the seventh millennium, or the seventh day, the Sabbath, which is a state where the light of the Creator fills the corrected properties with bounty and delight.

The number seven itself bears a great meaning in Kabbalah. The system that manages our world consists of seven parts. That is why things in our world are divided by seven or seventy: the seven days of the week, the seventy nations of the world, the seventy parts of humanity's soul, and the length of a human's life, lasting approximately seventy years.

The entire path of humankind consists of six days, representing the six thousand years of correction. We have now entered the year 5766 in the Jewish calendar. The Zohar points to the generation of the Messiah as the time when the conscious correction of the world should begin, and the Vilna Gaon (GRA), Rabbi Yitzhak Kook, as well as Baal HaSulam, all point to our generation as the generation of the Messiah. In the years we have left before the end of the six thousand years, the Jews and the whole of humankind must complete the correction, and in the seventh millennium, we will receive the reward for our world.

When you read these lines, you must wonder if there is a way to shorten our path toward the purpose of creation, to get to the correction sooner. The answer is that we not only can, but we *must* intervene in the process, which was meant to last seven thousand years, to accelerate it. Those who can reach this process individually will reach the upper world and the sensation of the complete and sublime reality before the others. But even during the process of correction, if we go through it consciously, through our own efforts, we will feel it as a creative process, a romantic desire.

ABRAHAM THE PATRIARCH

Just as the Creation story can be used to help us understand the evolution of our souls and our purpose on the earth, the story of Abraham the Patriarch teaches us about the essentials of growing toward the Creator and coming to know Him in our lives to fulfill our purpose in life. Anyone who ascends from this world toward the Creator and unites with Him must take the same path that Abraham first took, and for which he is regarded as the father of the nation. The following excerpts give us the inner meaning of Abraham's incredible journey:

Now the LORD said unto Abram: "Get thee out of thy country, and from thy kindred, and from thy father's house, unto the land that I will show thee. And I will make of thee a great nation, and I will bless thee, and make thy name great; and be thou a blessing. And I will bless them that bless thee, and him that curseth thee will I curse; and in thee shall all the families of the earth be blessed." So Abram went, as the LORD had spoken unto him; and Lot went with him; and Abram was seventy and five years old when he departed out of Haran. And Abram took Sarai his wife, and Lot his brother's son, and all their substance that they had gathered, and the souls that they had gotten in Haran; and they went forth to go into the land of Canaan; and into the land of Canaan (Gen. 12:1–5). And the LORD appeared unto Abram, and said: "Unto thy seed will I give this land"; and he built there an altar unto the LORD, who appeared unto him (Gen. 12:7). And there was a famine in the land; and Abram went down into Egypt to sojourn there; for the famine was sore in the land (Gen. 12:10).

The first question we may ask is: Why did the Creator choose Abraham? At that time, Abraham was no different from all the other people who lived in the area that spread from east of Syria to Mesopotamia. Furthermore, Abraham did not go to Egypt right away. Rather, he first went to Beit-El and offered a sacrifice to the Creator, and that seemed to soothe his mind. It is written that after that there was a famine, and only then did Abraham go down to Egypt. A question comes to mind: Was it the famine that made him go to Egypt, or was it the Creator?

If we relate to the Torah as a historic tale, we will see that it is not very different from the histories of other nations. But the Torah does not deal with the past, rather it deals with us. It deals with each and every one of us; with who we are and what we are and what we must do with our lives. The Creator appeals only to people, to each and every person. That is how the Torah explains the entire system of creation. Each person contains everything that exists in all the worlds inside him or her, including our own world. Besides humanity, there is only the Creator. Humanity is the representative of creation and of all the other worlds.

The Creator turns to Abraham, who represents a specific attribute in us and who is like all other properties (nations) in a human (*Av Ha'am*, Abraham in Hebrew, means "the father of the nation"), and tells him: "I now separate this specific trait in you, which is called Abraham, and you must leave your country, meaning your situation and all the desires that you currently feel. Go from your homeland, and break free from the desires you were born with."

In other words, God tells Abraham that he must exit his original state of being, the state he was born into. The Creator is inside Abraham's primary egoistic desires, and he must leave them and go to the land that God will show him. There is where Abraham will find God. (The words "that I will show thee" pertain to desires that the Creator will show Abraham and in which He will appear). The Creator only appears before Abraham to compel him to take the path at the end of which He will appear before him in completeness. In that state, the entire creation will appear before Abraham, and he will obtain the opposite properties: eternity and completeness and the degree of the Creator Himself.

The Creator appears before every single one of us just as He did before Abraham. We have all felt, even if only once in our lives, an inner voice, an inner power and desire to live in a different way—to think more of timeless, meaningful things, leaving behind all the petty dealings and routines of life and slowly rising above them, somehow leaping out of them.

As for Abraham, my intention is not to speak of him as a person who lived five thousand years ago, singled out by the

Creator. Rather, I would like to focus on the property of Abraham that is in each and every one of us. How does the Creator turn to this property and use it to attract us?

By telling Abraham to leave his desires, the substance in which he was created and had been immersed, and go to another desire, one that God will show him, the Creator does not show us that we must ascend spiritually. Rather, He says that we must first go down to Egypt, meaning to the gutter, to our darkest and fiercest egoistic desires. These desires are so egoistic that they are like the Egyptians in our world, who knew how to use the egoism so perfectly that they could mummify their bodies and preserve them virtually forever. They even made idols of their dead and were completely tied to their bodies.

The Creator does not tell Abraham that he must aspire upward to cross to the other desire, that there is where he will find the Creator and be filled with Him. That means that the most perfect state is when Abraham has already been through Egypt. The Creator doesn't even say that Abraham must go through Egypt, but simply tells him to go there. It is an unreasonable commandment. After all, Abraham is an ordinary person, a shepherd who lives his daily life in the bosom of his family. Suddenly he is compelled to experience terribly low situations (called Egypt) to attain the higher spiritual state. Abraham builds an altar, thanks the Creator for having noticed him, and remains in his place. Though Abraham goes to Beit-El, where he thinks he is closer to the Creator, the truth is that the Creator drives him away from there.

PERSONAL DEVELOPMENT IN THE FOOTSTEPS OF ABRAHAM

Abraham goes as far as Beit-El. This is likened to a person who attains spirituality and begins to be attracted to the books that concern that subject. He or she reads them, perhaps even begins to study Kabbalah, and thinks that this is Beit-El (house of the Lord). When Abraham sacrifices to the Creator—when he begins to examine what life really asks of him, what the Creator and his inner voice want him to do—he suddenly begins to feel hunger. That hunger is so intense that it drives him off to Egypt. During a preliminary reading of the books, we begin to feel ever-growing pains, accompanied by a still greater spiritual hunger. We begin to see ourselves through our innermost feelings as lower and meaner than ever. The world appears so petty, that this feeling is like going down to Egypt, meaning to our lowest desires.

The phase in which we are able to feel ourselves is the best and most vital for our progress. The intensity or quality of the sensation is of no importance; it can be good or bad, uplifting or depressing. We cannot obtain the correct desires, under the direct instruction of the Creator, without first being in Egypt. Our initial desires are very small, and even if we stretch them to the limit, they can only bring us as far as Beit-El, meaning the practice of the ordinary Torah, where we feel as if we have already entered the house of God, and the Garden of Eden and the next world are ready for us. But in fact, this is not the case! The Torah should bring us first to the recognition of evil, to the feeling that we are completely egotistical and that all our desires are completely opposite to spirituality. If we experience that state, understand and internalize it, then we accept that that is also our own situation. People's recognition of their ego must be an emotional, tangible experience. To the extent that they feel it this way, they begin to want to correct themselves. Therefore, the recognition of our ego as evil is a very long phase.

The exile in Egypt is not intended for Abraham, but rather for Jacob and his family (Josef and his brothers). The exile was meant to last four hundred years, but in fact it was shorter. Baal HaSulam writes that because they did not complete the four hundred years, the entire nation that left Egypt was forced to experience another exile, the one that has been ongoing for the past two thousand years.

To feel who you are and what your properties are, you must feel at least a little bit of what spirituality is like. You must experience these feelings to the fullest and examine them in every way. When the process is completed, you are granted exodus from Egypt.

Abraham only represents the first phase of this development. Once you begin to study the wisdom of Kabbalah, you feel much worse than before. However, this feeling is only the first entrance to Egypt, and it passes. Afterward Abraham returns to Beit-El. On his next journey to Egypt, he takes his family with him. This implies that he has accumulated a substantial amount of desires and has already acquired a clear notion of the way he must go toward spirituality. At this stage, he has already reached a certain degree of spiritual development and has already absorbed it. Only after that happens is he granted the second descent to Egypt.

Abraham immediately "went down to Egypt," but only reached as far as Beit-El, because we can only be pushed ahead by pain. Abraham was immersed in his egoistic desires. His country, family, and his father's house, the things and places he was commanded to leave behind, felt like his entire being. At first, Abraham thinks that he cannot leave behind those things (which in fact designate spiritual states) because they are his very nature, and he cannot imagine a different way of thinking, much less a different way of action.

We cannot imagine what is not within us to begin with, what we never felt, and even what our parents and our forebears never felt. Because of that, it is only possible to bring us out of that state and throw us into the state of acquiring new desires through immense spiritual hunger. That hunger can only be developed and amplified in a group with a teacher and some very special books. If we read these books in the wrong order, it is very easy to be misled and deviate from the right path, which means a temporary halt in spiritual evolution. We must always maintain a careful watch and examination, making sure we are on the right track. But in fact, even if we stand still, yet nevertheless desire spirituality, then the Creator Himself pushes us forward using that hunger.

Abraham represents a spiritual trait that seems to be the basis of all our traits. It is a general spiritual attribute that is the first to be approached by the Creator. People don't come to the wisdom of Kabbalah because they were sent here, but because the Creator approached them first. He begins to haunt them and make them hungry, and only then they come. One will never chase something without a reason or a special need for it. Only the sensation of hunger pushes us out of our metaphorical home country. Love and hunger, meaning the sensation of the absence of something, rule the world. That sensation is called Abram, and it is to that part of ourselves that the Creator turns to say: "Do you really want to fulfill your desires and attain the truth? If you do, you must leave this state of mind altogether and move on to another one called Egypt. That means that you really must see who you are and study your egoistic desires from within. If you correct them, you will attain Me; I will be revealed to you in them." The Creator appears precisely in those desires we call Egypt. Only after that are they corrected.

Let us take one more look at Abraham. In a different time and place, meaning in a different spiritual degree, we might have referred to him as a prophet. A prophet is a person who has attained such a spiritual degree that he or she is now in direct contact with the Creator. There are prophets who only speak to the Creator, meaning they attain the level of spiritual speech. Naturally, they do not hear any horns blowing in the sky, as the Torah writes, and the voice of God does not sound off from Mount Sinai from gigantic speakers to the whole of humankind. Rather, they hear the inner voice of one who obtains an evident contact with the Creator. There are prophets who see and hear, and there are those who only see and hear afterward. The books of the prophets demonstrate how versatile the connections of the prophets with the Creator are and how and when He appears before them, meaning in which spiritual degree one can reach which degree of prophecy.

The degrees of prophecy, as all other spiritual degrees of our forefathers, are all within us, and we experience each phase along the path of our development. We must go the entire way while being in our corporeal world. Everything that the Torah speaks of must be attained by us from beginning to end. Only then does one find oneself completely united with the Creator, having reached the final point of development, which constitutes the purpose of creation and its preliminary design. In fact, the Torah provides us with this entire plan, but tells us about it in a special way.

If the Creator turns to you, you feel it as that unique property called Abraham. That inner voice that you feel addresses you is called the Creator. The effort to understand it, the voice and indeed yourself, is what the Torah aspires for. Nothing more.

STAYING ON COURSE

Like the earth in the story of Genesis, the soul must go through a certain process of development in the body. It takes more than one lifetime to complete the process, meaning that the soul clothes itself in many bodies over many cycles. Although the process is clear, we can go our entire life without feeling that we have a soul, a spiritual component, thus not realizing the purpose of our life in this world.

As we have said, the soul is merely a desire to enjoy, to receive. It defines the attributes and the needs of the body, while the body itself is a dead object. The development of the soul creates different needs in the human being. Its desires change with its evolution from desires for bodily pleasures—food, sleep, and sex, just as in animals—to the desire to return to its spiritual state, the primary state from which it descended to this world.

Those desires do not evolve one at a time, but in a jumble. That is why a person can feel he or she has a craving for knowledge and at the same time a desire for money, honor, and sex. It happens in any person, because all the desires are made of a unique compound.

The same principle applies to the desire for spirituality. It can be revealed along with lower desires, but what distinguishes it is that we cannot satisfy it with anything mundane, because the source for this desire is outside our world. The revelation of such a desire testifies to the degree of development of the soul.

The souls return and descend to this world's bodies and develop over many lifetimes, until the moment when a person feels an attraction for something that is outside this world. Humanity undergoes various phases of development, and contemporary souls reveal desires for spirituality. In the past, such desires only appeared in distinguished individuals, but today we can see them surfacing in millions.

The process of developing of the desires can only happen in souls that are dressed in bodies, meaning in souls in this world. To receive infinite pleasures, wholeness, knowledge, and eternity, there has to be an independent desire for the pleasure and the sensation of its absence. That is why the primordial soul, as perfect as it was in its creation, could not appreciate its own perfection and had to descend to the lowest level, to our world, to rise from this low point and learn to appreciate the perfect state.

Because we are all parts of the same soul, any person must, either in this life or in a future one, develop to the point where he or she will begin to feel a desire for connection with the Creator or Upper One and return to the initial state from which his or her soul came and to which it must return. However, we must attain that preliminary state while still in this world, when our souls are clothed in a body. In the beginning, the soul was at its place, connected with its root, but denied of a body. The difference between that situation and the state when the soul is clothed in a body is that, in the latter, the soul attains a great deal more upper light and pleasure than it had in the preliminary state.

Even if a person does begin to feel a need to return to his or her spiritual root, that need is felt unconsciously. Hence, he or she undergoes further processes before the initial desire turns to a genuine desire that would actually be able to receive and appreciate the sublime pleasure, the perfect state.

Everything has a soul, not just humans and animals, but the vegetative and the inanimate as well. There is a good reason why humankind was created last in the chain of descent from above, meaning the worst with the greatest desire for pleasure. Compared to its root, human beings are the farthest creatures from spirituality. But precisely because they have great desires, they are able to overturn them and rise to attain spiritual attainment.

Our desire for spirituality is not a big one. We therefore have to intensify it to the point where we can be filled with the entire upper light and sublime delight. Our entire life's work, therefore, is to obtain a desire for spirituality that is greater than all other desires. To help us develop a desire to feel the perfect, eternal pleasure, an invisible light descends to our souls from our roots, which awakens in us new desires we do not understand.

It is that light that creates around us a certain environment, internal and external conditions that awaken in us the need to develop these desires, such as a hostile environment or a sensation of fear from an inner enemy inside us. If such feelings come to a person "out of the blue," it will be frightening. But if a person is made to understand, either directly or through

a messenger, that these external conditions were sent on purpose to awaken him or her to connect with the Upper One, that
person will not be afraid of these so-called enemies.

All kinds of unpleasant situations are sent to us so that we
will finally understand that it is not the external things that we
should fear, but the lack of contact with the Upper One, the
absence of spirituality. A complete desire for spirituality is built
gradually, by ascents and descents that come intermittently:
descents to desires of this world and ascents to desires of the
Upper One.

BECOMING A KABBALIST

If we cannot feel the upper world, it appears to us as though we
and the world have our own existence, and we cannot see how
much we ourselves and the world we live in are controlled from
above. This is the reason we feel that our surroundings are hostile and not a means to rush us back to our root.

Before the soul descends to the body, it is a small point in
its root. From there, the soul descends to our world, clothed in
a body, and loses contact with its root. It can return to its root
only if it annuls the bodily desires for worldly pleasures. There
are, all and all, 620 desires in the body. By correcting them, the
soul returns to its root, where it receives 620 times more pleasures than it had before its descent.

People who have crossed this road and accomplished this
correction are called Kabbalists. They live in our world and in
the spiritual root simultaneously. They tell us how to rise in
degrees that climb from this world back to our spiritual root.
When we read their explanations, we attract the illumination of
the upper light that pulls us forward.

All through the generations, Kabbalists have helped
humanity advance to its goal: the purpose of creation. But that
help was mostly secretive, "behind the scenes." Today, however,

because the desire for spirituality has already developed in millions, the Kabbalists clearly state that the help of the entire population is necessary to draw the spiritual light by the study of the wisdom of Kabbalah.

A soul that has attained contact with the Creator can perform much greater corrections in this world than the entire population can. When it performs corrections, it performs them through the public, which is why humanity must treasure such people. In spirituality, the work of the individual is more important than the work of the collective. Although both are important, it is impossible to compare them because they are entirely different kinds of spiritual work.

Kabbalists are in direct contact with spirituality, but they are also supported in their work by people. They raise people's desires to the spiritual world in such a way that they gather within them all the suffering of the collective society, and then raise it to the upper world. The Kabbalist receives bounty and light from the upper world, which descends on the people and shines on their lives in this world.

Though most people do feel pain, they are unaware of its purpose. If they could see what the feeling of pain creates in them, as Kabbalists do, they would not want to get rid of it, but only to correct it. A Kabbalist can actually feel the suffering of the public, but adds purpose to the suffering, and this way corrects it in the root.

Suffering is an unfulfilled need for spirituality. It is the reason for all the ailments in the world. The collective population feels pain in the form of suffering in our world—disease, poverty, and loss—while the Kabbalist transcends it to suffering, which stems from a lack of spiritual completeness.

We do not know the system of creation, and thus we use it incorrectly. It is as though a person must learn to manipulate a complex machine with many electronic, mechanic, hormonal, and nervous systems, as well as many other unknown systems that cannot be known or felt. That person presses the buttons before learning how to operate this machine.

The Kabbalists urge us to study to know how to operate the machine. We have to operate this machine, and that is the sole purpose for which we were created. That is precisely why we were given the freedom of choice, unlike the other creatures, to search the guidance of the Creator and justify it. When one has fully learned how to operate the "machine" of creation, thus completing the unification with the Creator, one replaces Him in the guidance of creation.

Leading creation is only possible when there is freedom of choice. If we do not participate in this leadership and do not realize the possibility to use our freedom of choice, and if we want to live like all other animals, then nature, meaning creation, continues to evolve by the same law that independently leads all of humankind and the universe to the goal. In this law, which brings all living things to the purpose of creation, to the best and most comfortable situation, there are two active forces: Judgment *(Din)* and Mercy *(Rachamim)*. As it says: "In the beginning God created the world with the attribute of *Din,* saw that the world could not exist, and associated it with the attribute of *Rachamim"* (Bereshit Raba 12:15).

It is our choice whether to advance to the purpose of creation independently, with the soft power of mercy, or leave things to nature, to the harsh force of judgment. In the end, what we must choose is whether to study Kabbalah, advance consciously to the goal, or not study and advance unconsciously, not knowing what is ahead of us. Only in that will we find our freedom.

This choice concerns all of us because our society is built like a pyramid. We complement each other's acts in the attempt to understand providence. Although the correction begins at the top, the preparation for it begins at the bottom, and if there is no willingness for correction below, it will be impossible to do anything above.

The conscious leadership of the world is intended for a chosen few, but the public has its own weight and can make a difference, though in a different way, through the study of the Kabbalah. As soon as it begins to ask about the surrounding world, it begins to change the world for the better.

There is no need for the entire world to obtain the knowledge of how every detail of reality works. Instead, the public must simply have the right approach to the conduct of reality and the purpose of creation. By doing that, it contributes its share to the efforts of the Kabbalists and complements them. It is enough if we hear, read, and speak of the existence of an upper force that leads us and upon which we depend. We have a special task, which is to take upon ourselves the leadership of the world and determine our future by ourselves—each person individually and the public as a whole. It is the duty of the public to raise the importance and the knowledge of the upper force above ground level.

Rabbi Akiva said that the entire Torah is comprised of one law: "Love thy neighbor as thyself." Twenty-four thousand of his disciples, who were taught to follow that law, still developed unfounded hatred for one another. All except five died because of that corruption; the ones who survived were those who were not dragged into hatred. Among them was Rabbi Shimon Bar-Yochai. When the disciples were united with love, it was called a time of the Temple. And when the corruption of unfounded hatred appeared, when they only had the will to receive for themselves, it was called the ruin of the Temple—first came the spiritual ruin and then the physical ruin that resulted from it. Anything that happens in our universe is a result of events that occur in the upper world and cascades to ours.

Kabbalists had foreseen the ruin of the Temple, and today they are trying to convince people to choose life, because they see a future catastrophe in spirituality. People believe that an evil thought can kill. Science also has learned that if a person with bad intentions approaches a plant, even though he or she may water the plant, ostensibly acting positively toward it, the plant will react to the negative attitude. That attitude can even be measured by how negative the reaction of the plant was, how much it was afraid and rejected that person.

It is becoming increasingly apparent, in every field of science and technology, that the stronger the energies, the more concealed they are. Science now begins to realize that our thoughts, not our actions, have the most powerful influence on the world. We can already hear scientists proclaiming that in the most delicate experiments the identity of the researcher is of vital importance, because the reaction of the substance and the outcome of the experiment depend on the moral level of the researching scientist.

In all the holy books, not a single word is mentioned about this world, only about the spiritual world. These books are called "holy" because holiness means bestowal, the attribute of the Creator. In the Torah, the entire process of creation is explained in words of this world, as well as the entire process of the soul's correction, until we reach the purpose of creation, the degree of the Creator.

3

THE EVOLUTION OF THE SOULS

The development of humankind over thousands of years is a realization of different levels of desire. The search for ways of fulfilling these emerging desires determines this or that level of civilization's evolution and everything we define as technological and scientific progress.

Because desires constantly improve, evolve from smaller to bigger, humankind advances. Kabbalah divides the entire complex of human desires into five stages:

- Primary stage or still degree: need for sex and food

- Second stage or vegetative degree: striving for riches

- Third stage or animate degree: craving for power and fame

- Fourth stage or speaking degree: thirst for knowledge

- Fifth stage or speaking within the speaking degree: aspiration to spirituality, to the Creator

The need for sex and food are the same desires as those of animals. Even in complete isolation, we would still feel hunger and the urge to reproduce, to have sexual relations.

Desires for wealth, power, fame, and knowledge are human desires, since to satisfy them one must be surrounded by other people.

We are born, our animal and human desires develop, and then we find out that their realization does not satisfy us, since our secret but true aspiration, which we cannot yet realize and formulate, falls outside the boundaries of this world.

We receive this desire from above. It is neither given by nature as animal desire, nor does it develop under the influence of a society as do human desires. Kabbalah calls this level of desire "the desire for spiritual light" or "the soul."

Kabbalah studies the spiritual construction named "the collective soul" or "Adam." This construction consists of 600,000 parts, each of them splitting into a multitude of fragments, located inside our earthly desires.

EMERGENCE OF A NEW KIND OF DESIRE

The sum total of earthly desires is called "the heart." The fragment (desire), placed in the heart from above, is referred to as "a point in heart."

During our biological lives in this world, we should completely fulfill our spiritual desire. We will keep returning to our world until this goal is reached. Thus, each generation in our world constitutes the same 600,000 souls, vested in the bodies of our world.

Each generation is the same 600,000 souls progressing forward to be filled by Supreme Light. The body dies, and the soul moves on and dresses in a new body, works in it again for the sake of being filled, until at a certain stage of development it will be filled with the Supreme Light.

Most people feel only the needs limited by the framework of our world. These include creative, intellectual, and cultural aspirations and the need to research and understand the structure of our world. This indicates that souls dressed in the bodies of these people have not yet reached a desire for spirituality—the fifth stage of our desire's development. Souls of this type do not harbor aspirations to develop beyond their worldly bodies.

However, there are souls of a different type. Being installed in a protein body, such souls force one to long for something unearthly and eternal. Like others, these people try to be satisfied with what this world can provide, but to no avail. They see how other people crave for riches and success and realize it is no more than a game. They participate in these "games," often with success, but it brings them no satisfaction.

Gradually, disappointed and disenchanted, those people begin to feel that their souls demand a different kind of satisfaction. They feel that they can no longer fulfill themselves with earthly pleasures, that their life is empty. In that state they begin to look for the way to fulfill the new, spiritual desire.

Search and disappointment are the highlights of this new kind of desire, so characteristic of our time. Beginning in the middle of the twentieth century, more and more people have begun to awaken to this spiritual desire sent from above. Being combined with all other desires, it creates a conflict in the heart. The fifth desire causes inner discomfort and ultimately leads a person to Kabbalah.

However, since the spiritual desire descends from above, it cannot be filled with objects of our world. Kabbalah teaches how this most exalted desire can be filled. Kabbalists, who fill this spiritual desire, call this filling light, or rather, the Supreme Light. They name the desire for spiritual fulfillment "a point in the heart."

THE POINT IN THE HEART

Anyone who longs to attain the attributes of the Creator and unite with Him is called *Yehudi* (Jewish), from the Hebrew word *Yechudi* (unique), to signify the act of unification with the Creator. If a person has that desire, then Kabbalah deals with its realization. If there is no desire, that person will never approach Kabbalah in the first place. That is why there is no coercion in spirituality, and there is no commitment to practice it. Only those who have a desire will approach Kabbalah, which testifies to the fact that their time has come to draw near the Creator.

All souls are parts of a single collective soul, but each of them develops at its own pace. That is why there are souls that demand spiritual development right now, and then there are souls that can wait. Most souls are still developing within the framework of our world.

An individual cannot impose on him- or herself the desire for spirituality. Rather, he or she wishes for different things in this life and at a very unexpected moment a desire for spirituality awakens. This is called "the point in the heart"—a seed, the embryo of the soul. When that happens, the person begins to search and continues to do so until he or she finds the wisdom of Kabbalah.

If a person is still at the stage when he or she hasn't come to realize where to proceed and why but only feels a vague desire for spirituality, it might take years and perhaps lifetimes before he or she comes to Kabbalah. That will be the case with the whole of humankind, as the prophet Jeremiah says: "For they shall all know Me, from the least of them unto the greatest of them" (31:33). Thereby, imposing the wisdom of Kabbalah on anyone is simply impossible.

THE SCIENCE OF KABBALAH

The Kabbalah is a science that studies the system of creation, the way it was formed, the root of its essence and its structure. It examines how the Creator conducts this system and how creation should correct itself to rise to the degree of the Creator, which is in fact the purpose of creation. Kabbalah is a science that deals with drawing near to the Creator, whereas religion simply indicates to people what they should do with the protein bodies of our world. The wisdom of Kabbalah has no connection with any popular religious movements.

The Baal Shem Tov created the movement of Hasidism to help the Jewish orthodox person integrate a certain amount of spiritual intention in the performance of the physical Mitzvot (commandments). However, the Baal Shem Tov was first and foremost a Kabbalist of the highest degree. He therefore established Hasidism as a popular movement in order to select out of the masses the few people who had the desire and the ability to become Kabbalists. This way he managed to find disciples who later became the first *Admorim* (Jewish masters and teachers), who went on to establish their own trends in Hasidism and beyond. The task of the movement was to select the individuals who wanted to attain the Creator from the collective and render certain support to the general public.

A Kabbalist is a person who studies the system of creation through inner efforts. This person looks deeply into him- or herself and performs actions called *tikkunim* (corrections). This way he or she climbs the ladder of the spiritual worlds to the end of correction, to complete equivalence of form with the Creator and total adhesion with Him. That can only be attained through the wisdom of Kabbalah, and only a person who has already been awakened to spirituality can come to that. The Baal Shem Tov assumed that if he imparted the public with a basic knowledge in the wisdom of Kabbalah through the movement of Hasidism, the ones who sensed the points in their hearts would finally come to him.

All people will eventually come to feel that they need spiritual elevation, but it is a gradual process. All ailments and pains in the world stem from misusing the will to receive. Hence, all people need is the knowledge of how to use their spiritual and corporeal desires correctly. The wisdom of Kabbalah explains to people how to use their desires in the most effective way to benefit themselves, their family, and the whole of humankind now and for all times.

INTERPRETING THE SPIRITUAL COMPASS

To research itself and the surroundings, humanity has developed various sciences such as physics, chemistry, biology, and so on. These are called the natural sciences, and they are based on our five senses. To help ourselves study nature, we have built instruments that extend the range of our senses. Gradually, from generation to generation, we have gained experience and reached a better understanding of the problem of survival in this world. But among all sciences, there is one that develops us quite differently—the science of Kabbalah.

Beyond the corporeal world that we research, there is another world, which is concealed. Though we cannot see it, we do feel its existence. But if it is invisible, how can we assume that this other world really exists? It is because we see that there are specific laws, which are a part of a broader reality. We understand that such general, more rational laws, which describe our lives and our existence comprehensively, simply must exist. There is something that eludes us, something around us we cannot grasp. But how can we come to grasp it if we don't have the appropriate senses? Can we create them, or acquire them, to feel a more complete and real creation?

It is quite possible that this alternate creation does exist around us in all its layers, but we divide it into the apprehended part we call "our world" or "this world," and the as-yet-unfelt layer. If we had other senses, although it's hard for us to imagine it, we would probably also feel the world differently, perhaps with a broader and deeper vision. But such senses don't exist, and so we suffer. We don't know how to behave with one another and with our surroundings because we don't see our past and future lives.

When dealing with a scientific study of the world, we come to a stage where our knowledge is exhausted, and we're left helpless. Though there are many ways to enhance our ability to predict the future, beyond the boundaries of our regular senses, they in fact add very little to our understanding of the world. We are capable of attaining very limited abilities to predict events, but we never achieve clear knowledge of the future and complete attainment, which can only happen when we are acting in full cooperation with the world around us.

The human being is a highly developed creature. But the more humanity develops, the more individuals feel helpless and lost. We see that the development of science and research into the world around us has failed to give us the results we were hoping for. Hence, we must face the fact that the solution to the problem is found in our senses themselves. A very accurate method we can use to develop an additional sense is called the "screen" or "returning light." The screen, which is in essence a sixth sense, gives us the ability to see and feel that part of reality we can't perceive with our normal senses.

We receive our five senses at birth, but we ourselves must develop the sixth sense. This happens when an individual is suddenly "summoned" from above and feels compelled to experience a more comprehensive reality, and thus the need to develop the sixth sense is born. This is a gradual process. Humanity is constantly evolving, and its desires, as well as

those of the individual, change continuously. At first, they aim
at physical pleasures on an animal level—the enjoyment of food,
sex, and family ties. Then, they desire satisfaction on a human
level, seeking wealth, power, respect, and knowledge. Only after
all those desires are realized does the desire to attain the sublime
reality appear, an essence beyond the physical world.

The first prompting to sense a reality beyond ourselves is
called the "embryo" of the sixth sense. From this stage on, the
development of the sixth sense will depend on the individual
alone. That sense cannot be developed in isolation, but rather
via a special system that has been given to humanity called "the
wisdom of Kabbalah."

In each generation, there are people who receive a prompting from above and feel the need to develop this sixth sense.
Then, somehow, these people find the books and the teachers
who can help them develop. These teachers are called
Kabbalists (from the word *lekabel,* to receive), because they
receive that knowledge and convey it to us so that we, too, can
attain their degree of spirituality. They speak of the way an
individual acquires the desire to attain the actual reality, after
he or she has already realized desires for wealth, power, respect,
and knowledge.

In the end, we must all come to a state (if not in this life,
then in the next) where we live simultaneously on all levels of
reality. We must feel this not only through our five senses, as we
all do, but through the new sense as well. This will ensure our
inner peace and complete tranquility.

The development of that inner vessel, the sixth sense, is
formed by the order of cause and effect, or by the pyramid principle, on which the whole of humankind is built. The sixth
sense is awakened in a certain type of person, one who is at the
top of the pyramid.

The people who first developed this sixth sense were called
Hebrews, from the Hebrew word *ever,* meaning to go over the

barrier, the border between our world and the spiritual world. Abraham the Patriarch was the first to cross over from the limited sensation of this world to the sensation of the upper world. The descendants of Abraham are therefore at the top of the pyramid in which the sixth sense will develop. But this is only the beginning of humanity's development. The prophets say that in the future all people will have to attain that higher level of development, a bonding with the upper forces and full comprehension of the life cycle. Everyone will have to attain an existence beyond the concepts of life and death as we know them and will then exist at all levels of reality.

All past Kabbalists have pointed to our time in history as the turning point, when millions of people would begin to adapt themselves to the spiritual realm and develop a sixth sense. Previous generations were in essence a preparation for this turning point. Those generations went through a process called "the decline of the souls," in which the soul descends from its uppermost state in the world of *Ein Sof* (endless world or infinity) and goes lower and lower, through many worlds, down to our own. Then, once in our world, the soul continues to descend through the generations, through the ruin of the first and second Temples and the four exiles. In our generation, the long exile has ended. From now on, there is only an ascent of souls.

All the Kabbalists before our time were people who prepared the system of the ascent for us. We, in our generation, are the group of souls that has joined together to become the first in the line of the collective group of souls to rise with our vessels, to actually elevate ourselves spiritually.

If you study the texts of the Ari and the books of Baal HaSulam, you will find that they say everything very simply. For this reason, the Kabbalah is beginning to be more open and more widely publicized in our time. Even so, only a handful of us understand what Kabbalah is really about, why it is called a science, why it was concealed, and why it comes to people in such a unique way.

When a person develops a clear need to understand the upper reality, he or she must start developing the point in the heart and the sixth sense by using the system of Kabbalah. This process takes several years. The sixth sense grows slowly and evolves; the individual begins to feel the outer world, the world of causality. He or she is then given a precise vision of the reasons for events in our world and is able to see the origins and conclusions of all acts, all forces, all our desires and thoughts.

The "self" of a person, that which belongs to his or her essence, is felt only in the sixth sense. From the moment that sense develops, the individual begins to feel what we call the "soul." We are rewarded in two ways for this development. First, we begin to see how thoughts and desires pass from ourselves to others, understanding how we receive thoughts from others or are influenced by them. We begin to see how the world works, and how everything relates to the surrounding nature and returns back to us. The concept of time vanishes altogether, and we see everything—past, present, and future— at once, the real meaning of the word *time*.

The second reward is that the individual starts to acquire a correct understanding of what is happening around him or her, acquiring the ability to influence providence and to influence the world from the outside. Thus it is possible not only to predict the future, but also to *create* the future. These forces appear in us to the extent that we go beyond our own nature and begin to think in terms of the upper world.

All these things are real, and all of us, without exception, can attain them. The collective law of creation makes it necessary for each of us to advance to that state. However, humanity is walking toward this reality unconsciously, against its will. A person who begins to advance willingly toward the goal and who wishes to attain actual reality and the spiritual life no longer feels worldly pains and pressures, but immediately sees that nature and the universe are filled with good, not evil.

CREATOR AND CREATURE

Reality consists of two elements: Creator and creature. We feel this in our senses in various ways, but it is unchanging in and of itself. The sensation of the Creator is what we call "the world," or "creation." The creature can sometimes sense that the Creator is being partially or fully revealed; at other times He is altogether concealed. The creature may even lack awareness of the Creator altogether. The extent of awareness of the Creator depends solely on the creature, because the Creator, like the sun, never stops shining.

The Creator has the attributes of (bestowal) and benevolence. When the creature acquires these Creator-like attributes, this state is called equivalence of form with the Creator. The individual then senses the Creator as fully revealed, to the exact degree that his or her attributes resemble those of the Creator. When the attributes of a person are incompatible with those of the Creator, he or she feels the Creator as concealed. When these attributes oppose those of the Creator's, the individual feels the Creator does not even exist.

The creature feels the Creator as pleasure, as wisdom and peace and wholeness. Therefore, the intensity of those sensations depends on the intensity of the sensation of the Creator. The Creator formed all the creatures from an egoistic desire to enjoy. The Creator is perceived by the creature as pleasure in all its manifestations. Pleasure means the sensation of the Creator, or the light of the Creator, which are actually one and the same.

A creature is in essence a desire to delight in the Creator. The closer I feel to the Creator, the greater is my enjoyment. The further He is from me, the less I enjoy, until my sensations are turned to pain. We ourselves determine the extent to which we feel close to the Creator. We do that by changing our attributes. The closer our attributes become to the Creator's attribute of benevolence, the closer we become to Him. This is when we feel best. Thus, in fact, an individual changes his or her own destiny and becomes a partner in the leadership of the world.

The "world" is the sum total of all the conditions that define the measure of a person's equivalence or adhesion with the Creator. This degree of attachment is determined by us. We set the conditions for equivalence through our own will, through our intentions and prayers, all of which come from our desire. This process of directing our desires is called raising MAN (an Aramaic acronym for *Mayim Nukvin*—female water), the one factor by which the creature can influence his or her relationship with the Creator and what he or she will receive from above.

When a person is born into this world, the sense for perceiving the Creator is covered with a screen, which completely hides the Creator. Because of this screen, we cannot feel the presence of the Creator. What one does feel is called the "world," what one does not feel seems virtually nonexistent. The Creator is not concealed from me, but I, with my senses, do not feel Him. Perhaps I even conceal Him, because what I feel is not Him, but the screens that conceal Him. I can, however, influence my relationship with Him, breaking through these screens.

When the first Jewish farmers began to populate the Negev desert in the south of Israel, Rav Yehuda Ashlag was asked, "Wherever will they get water?" He answered that the water would come through the prayer of the farmers. He was then told that the farmers were secular and even opposed to religion, so how then would they pray? To that he replied: "It is of no importance. Any man's desire for life is sensed by the Creator, who is the source of all life, and therefore, the Creator will grant them their wish, even if they are unaware of it." This means that, no matter what, our desire rises up to the Creator and always has an effect, even though we may not know of the existence of the Creator or feel Him, even if we deny Him, don't understand His actions, or fail to justify Him altogether.

THE POWER OF A DIRECTED DESIRE

The Creator creates the desire, which is a given constant. It rises from below, within us, and surfaces in various intensities. The aim, however, is to change the desire from a corrupted wish to receive for the self alone to a corrected desire to receive for the sake of the Creator. Even an ordinary person, one who is not a Kabbalist, can raise MAN through thoughts, desires, and aims, because there is always a desire in his or her mind to receive from the Creator, though he or she may not even recognize the Creator's existence.

This mission can be achieved by thought, aim, and will. We are all obligated to fulfill it, regardless of our social, financial, or religious status. Everyone must know that destiny can be changed only by our inner acts.

We must turn to the upper force and approach Him. The very nearness is enough. The Creator's light, which draws us all toward Him, is, to the creatures, the one and only law of creation. This gravitating force first affects the Jews, and then the rest of the nations. The force awakens us, through pain, to make us approach Him. When a person fails to want the Creator independently, he or she is pushed to it by pain. We will be at ease only if we avoid this force before it acts on us, by drawing ourselves toward the Creator of our own accord. This is called progress in the "path of light," as opposed to progress in the "path of pain."

Our situation depends solely on how we relate to the upper force that pulls us toward it. It is not a question of politics, and attempts to please our enemies will not do us any good either. Our situation depends not on our willingness to practice the regular Mitzvot (precepts), because the Creator wants the heart, not a mechanical act. We must attain the spiritual degrees of the precepts, meaning to keep the law of creation in the spirit. It is impossible to keep a spiritual law as though it were a mechanical law, because to truly keep a spiritual law means to equalize with it, to be inside it, and to be identical with it. The Creator and the entire spiritual world are a single giving force. Humans must come to resemble it, meaning correct all their desires to be used only for bestowal upon the Creator, just as all the Creator wants is to bestow goodness upon humans.

The human soul consists of 613 desires. In the beginning they are egoistic desires, but if one corrects them to be used to bestow contentment upon the Creator, this act of correction is called a Mitzvah. The Light enters the corrected desire, and this is called "the revelation of the Creator," or "the Light of the Torah." When all the desires are corrected in order to bestow pleasure upon the Creator, it is a state known as *dvekut* (adhesion) with Him, and the Creator fills the creature, or appears before the creature. That state of unification is called "Israel, the Torah, and the Creator, are one."

If your desire for the Creator is stronger than the force with which He pulls you to Him, then you are in spirituality and possess your own spiritual screen, your own spiritual power. That means that there is a screen over your egoism, and your attraction to the Creator is through your desire to give to Him, rather than to take for yourself.

To remain in this state of spirituality a person must strain to act against his or her own nature every second. There is no such concept in spirituality as resting or pausing or doing nothing. A person must constantly strive to increase his or her efforts, a need that stems from the need to give, to bestow.

If, however, a person's desire does not grow, he or she falls into the hands of the *Sitra Achra* (Aramaic for the "other side"), the system of the dark forces, impurity. It is here, and only here, that we have freedom of choice, and that is given to us from above. The moment we can no longer make an effort, our freedom is denied, and the attitude toward us from above immediately becomes utterly negative. The Creator becomes concealed, and individuals begin to feel that their environment—nature, society, and their enemies—are placing obstacles in their way. But nature and society and enemies are only costumes of the Creator. The more a person deviates from his or her desire to focus on the center, the law that brings the whole of creation to the center acts on one more forcefully.

Because humankind continues to evolve, the collective law of nature, which aspires to centralize everything, demands a greater effort and deeper awareness from those who are more developed. If an individual does not promptly make this effort, he or she will instantly pay a penalty, having to make greater efforts and suffer greater pains, and then more effort and more pain and so on.

In the beginning of the twentieth century, humanity thought good times had come, and that we would be able to enjoy our many discoveries. But at the close of the century, we saw how much torment humanity had experienced. In addition, environmental catastrophes, disintegration of the family unit, escape to drugs, and worldwide terrorism have all escalated. All this is a result of the human ego that grows without any correction. The upper force must bring us to a point where we will find it necessary to correct our nature.

The way to correct the world is by using the method of Kabbalah. This is why it is appearing in our time, and this is why now there is a desire for it in the world. The people of Israel have an obligation to keep their task as chosen people and to be a light to the nations by bringing correction to the world through the wisdom of Kabbalah.

For example, when tragedy befalls us, we have to understand that it is the Creator who sends it, trying to get us to focus on Him. That, in fact, is our work against the fear for our lives. The very instant we fall under the influence of pain, or pleasure, we must keep in mind that it comes from the Creator.

The settlers in the Negev desert asked for rain and got it, although they were not crying for the Creator. If they had turned to Him consciously, of their own choice, they would have received a whole river running in the middle of the desert. But the time of mercy is now over; we have grown too much, and the law that brings us back to the goal demands of us to turn to the Creator consciously and purposefully.

And here begins the process of *Lo Lishma* (not for Her name), the process for myself. I begin in a situation where I tell myself: "I want to live, therefore I must turn to the upper force." Then the law that brings us back to the goal of creation demands of us to know to whom we plead: "I want to live therefore I must turn to the upper force, but I have to know how to turn to Him." Hence the necessity for Kabbalah, and the light in it, which reforms and brings us back to our root and gives us the desire *Lishma* (for Her name), the desire to give to the Creator.

People will not have to change anything in their lives to receive this light. The only thing the Creator wants is contact with His creatures that is just a little better than the one He had with the farmers in the Negev. He wants a conscious bond aimed at Him alone.

The next phase of development is the attainment of a bilateral contact wherein a person says to God, "I not only expect something of You, but I want to see You in everything that happens to me; I know that You are the one hiding in the picture of the world before me. I am not hiding from You, I want to be good to You, so that You will be good to me."

It takes nothing more than a desire to be in that kind of contact with the Creator to reach the top of the pyramid with the Kabbalists. Today, everyone must know about this work. We have already come so far that each person will discover how the Creator is clothed in each of us.

PROPER DEVELOPMENT

The evolution of humankind on an egoistic basis (for myself alone) caused the creation of a deep chasm between the moral level of humanity and the technological level it reached. That is exactly what Plato and Aristotle feared when they prohibited the study of sciences to those of unworthy moral standards.

There is not a shadow of a doubt that there is a connection between the moral degree of a person, meaning their intentions, and their scientific ability. Without the intent to discover the Creator and understand the purpose of creation, scientific studies only reveal a certain aspect of the laws of reality and how they work in our narrow world. After all, we study reality from an egoistic perspective, and therefore we perceive only certain connections out of all the details of our surrounding reality.

Each law acts in all the realms of creation, in this world and in the spiritual world. But we can see its full range of operation only if we too are in a realm that encircles the whole of creation. For that we must be compatible with the attributes of the realm we want to encircle—altruistic attributes of giving, the attributes of the degrees of the upper worlds.

We do not change nature on our own. The attributes of nature never change, and there is also no change in the interconnections between the forces of nature. But nature looks different according to the attributes of its researcher. Nature shows a different aspect, not a different law, and we understand only what we perceive and feel through our five senses. Hence, our feeling is forever personal and subjective.

Because all people have a common nature, we perceive the world in the same way at first. Nature remains unchanged, but when we change ourselves, we feel that nature's laws operate differently on us. We change the way we are exposed to the laws of nature. That is why Malachi says, "I the Lord do not change" (3:6). It is indeed surprising that we can change the things around us, when in fact nothing really changes but ourselves. We feel as though nature changes because of the change within.

Nature is the law of gravity, the laws of chemistry and physics, and so on. These laws do not change with our personal evolution. What does change is not how the laws work, but how we perceive them, how we feel the change in the sensations that we perceive. However, we think that the change happens outside us because we are built to regard ourselves as the unchanging center of creation.

Only one state is complete perfection, and by changing our attributes, we approach that state and feel it more and more clearly. Thus, the only processes that actually take place in creation are processes of inner change in our attributes. And it is within that change that we feel as though providence is changing toward us.

Therefore, we must know how to change our inner attributes so that we can change the laws of nature in our favor. When we learn how to do that, we will be certain of the result, of our tomorrow. But the wisdom of Kabbalah tells us that that change depends on our refusal to use our egoism.

As science progresses, scientists are beginning to find that we can influence the phenomena of nature. They have found that the result of a scientific experiment depends on the personal attributes of the researcher. Of course, there are also experiments where the researcher is of no importance—regardless of the researcher's intentions, the result will be the same. But there is a finer level in nature, above substance, where the result is affected by the personal attributes of the researcher.

We will soon see that it is not enough to equip scientists with the most sophisticated instruments. There will be a real need for scientists who are "taught" to influence nature the right way, because we influence nature by simply being in it. The only question is: What is the right kind of influence? It might be that in the next stage of evolution, science will no longer need mechanical, electronic, or optic instruments or devices that enlarge or miniaturize objects, but the individual him- or herself will be the instrument that will research nature and will know how to influence the world correctly, to bring about the most desirable results.

The science concerned with the linkage between our influence on nature and the outcome that we get back from it is the science of Kabbalah. It teaches us how our actions and our influence on nature yield this or that result. Like any other science, Kabbalah also uses exact terms and a completely scientific language.

In scientific research, we want to receive from nature around us the necessary information for our survival and all the other things that we need. In the near future, it will be enough to activate one's personal attributes to attain all that, instead of all the devices and the mechanisms we have invented.

INTENTION AND CHANGE

Kabbalah explains which attributes we must acquire to research reality correctly and helps us acquire the spiritual attributes with which we can influence the world. Kabbalah exposes us to the entire reality and explains its laws; it teaches us how we can influence the system of creation positively and get the best result in return. The method of our bestowal upon the surroundings is called the *kavana* (intention).

The further humanity evolves without fitting into the ultimate reality meant for it, the further the world submerges into a state of suffering and uncertainty. Therefore, in our current situation, Kabbalah is becoming a practical must.

The wisdom of Kabbalah is the discovery of the laws and the collective mechanism of reality. To a person living in our world, this is called the revelation of the Creator to His creatures. The revelation gives us the ability to approach the useful and stay away from the harmful and to know the reason for the good as well as the bad.

The purpose of the study of Kabbalah and its implementation is to attain the best possible results for humanity. The goal is simple: to attain happiness and peace both in the body and outside it, to attain eternity and wholeness. And isn't that what everyone is searching for?

The wisdom of Kabbalah also teaches us to manage the collective mechanism of creation in which our universe is but a tiny particle. Just as scientists study the phenomena and the laws of this world perceived by and apparent to all, so the Kabbalist scientists research the reality that is not perceived by our five senses and its laws.

We badly need this research because we are the only active beings in the whole of creation. Using the ordinary means at our disposal, we can only expose a tiny fraction of the surrounding reality, whereas the science of Kabbalah gives us the opportunity to study the entire reality, the entire system of creation, and to operate it.

Kabbalah reveals the collective thought of creation and the interrelationships between the various parts of creation. It teaches us of humankind's evolution in this world, what happens to our souls when we die, and how we come back to new bodies. It reveals what exists outside our lives during our reincarnations.

As a result of the study of Kabbalah, one learns how the mechanism of the management of creation works. Because of that, we learn how to behave correctly in every situation in life and affect the mechanism that determines our fate.

The very fact that we think and search for the way to influence the world for the better is, by itself, a great *tikkun* (correction). Every desire is a prayer to the Creator, even if one is unwilling to recognize the existence of the Creator.

Humanity has always sought to know the future, but no one has found an accurate method to predict it. What we are really looking for is a way to make ourselves feel good. We seek out all those sorcerers, magicians, and so-called Kabbalists, but so far we have failed to find the cure for our pains throughout our tormented history. But we can help ourselves! We must only learn to manage our own lives. For that we must first acquire the knowledge and the ability to influence nature.

There is a good reason why it takes a person between twenty and thirty years to grow, during which time he or she is placed under the care of nature and society. Only after maturation does nature become harsh with us. In fact, for us to assume the management of the world, we must acquire a spiritual screen (the aim to bestow), and then the Creator will endow us with the power to manage our own lives and the world around us in accordance with the strength of our screen.

A person with a screen controls his or her own destiny. Such a person acquires a force that is above his or her own life. That person can do anything that the upper degree demands. The ability to follow the directions of the upper degree instead of one's own mind is the one possibility for us to attain genuine freedom—control in our lives and a freedom of choice. We acquire the ability to receive powers from an upper degree and in this way rise to the upper degree by ourselves.

It is only possible to justify and understand the natural law (the Creator) at the end of this journey. Even in the midst of our lives, working toward this goal, we cannot justify such punishments as death and an incarnation into a new body. Only from a perspective higher than our own is it possible to justify what nature does with us. Every time a person is exposed to the influence of a higher degree, he or she must accept its reason and justify it. The ability to act against one's own mind and accept the reason of the Upper One is called "faith above reason."

We choose between the path of light (Kabbalah) and the path of pain, depending on how we relate to our evolution, whether it is within reason or above reason. Only Kabbalists can actively intervene in the upper management, and yet, anyone who wishes to do well and give of him- or herself triggers a positive response in the upper world. Therefore, if the whole nation aspires to keep the collective law of creation, it will find it in the words "Love thy neighbor as thyself," a law that is no more and no less than the "law of love." But for this to happen, we must move beyond our emotions and thoughts, which are all based on our basic corporeal nature.

DEGREES OF DESIRE

Our task is to attain the highest degree in our advancement toward the Creator. That is the purpose of creation. The ladder between the Creator and us consists of 125 degrees or steps, also called desires. Each desire constitutes a complete and separate degree and is different in each stage of development. However, our own world does not constitute a degree of spiritual desire and is therefore excluded from the count of the 125 degrees. The 125 degrees begin only one step above our world, starting with the first degree of the spiritual world, and so on until the end of the 125th degree. What characterizes a higher degree is a greater desire to give and be altruistic.

The range of spiritual degrees is also divided into five worlds: the worlds of *Adam Kadmon,*[1] *Atzilut,*[2] *Beria,*[3] *Yetzira,*[4] and *Assiya.*[5] Each of these worlds is also comprised of five *partzufim,* and each *partzuf* is divided into five *sefirot.* Thus, the entire structure consists of 125 degrees (5 by 5 by 5). The worlds, the *partzufim,* and the *sefirot* define desires, their power, and spiritual degrees in ascending order.

In our world there are events that occur to each of us as individuals and events that occur to entire collectives, but the sole purpose of those events is to motivate us toward the barrier in our spiritual development, to cross it and start advancing in spirituality.

Each spiritual degree defines all our thoughts and desires, our entire spiritual being. When a person moves from one degree to the next, everything inside him or her changes as well. Each new degree controls us, and we are under its absolute control. It is impossible to go from one degree to another before the first one is attained completely.

At this point it is worthwhile to examine the purpose for which the light works on us. Aside from the desire itself, there is only the Creator, the light. The light is the sensation of the Creator, the sensation of life, both in our world and in the spiritual world. That light also has a power that can raise one to a higher degree. Therefore, certain operations were set up that we must perform, and through them, we draw this elevating light to us.

To summarize, the soul is the only creature that the Creator created, and that exists outside Him. It was created with an egoistic attribute, completely opposite from the Creator. Its necessitated end is to acquire the same nature as the Creator, meaning total altruism, and it is to do so over many life cycles of clothing human bodies.

The corrupted (egoistic) state is called "this world," and the corrected (altruistic) state is called "the world *Ein Sof*" (endless world). All the souls must reach the state of *dvekut* (adhesion, unity) with the Creator. The souls of Israel are called "chosen" because they have the task of correcting themselves first, before the souls of the other nations of the world, thus becoming "a light to the nations."

4

WHY NOW IS THE TIME

For two thousand years, the study of Kabbalah was forbidden to women and men under age forty, and there was a reason for this restriction. In fact, all the books of Kabbalah, including the Torah (the Pentateuch), were written only for our time, when everyone needs to practice the science of Kabbalah. What we should all do now is open the Kabbalah books and begin to learn how to attain the upper world. In this chapter, we will explore why now is the time to open these books and how to do so.

Kabbalists have expressed their frustration at the fact that we are still not using the study of Kabbalah as a springboard for the attainment of the upper worlds, since that is the one key to the gate of spirituality, the knowledge and the understanding of the wisdom of the upper world, which means eternal life, happiness, wholeness, and bounty for all humankind

Kabbalah is a science with clear and concise laws that must be studied. It has no connection with charms and blessings and other things that are done in its name, originating in the time Kabbalah was concealed from people and ascribed magical forces. The books of Kabbalah clearly explain what steps we need to take to acquire that knowledge.

The special thing about genuine books of Kabbalah is that they are suitable for all and contain the connection between the soul of the person who is studying them and the upper worlds, from which that person's soul originates. The books direct us to develop in our own unique way, according to our inner structure and the root of our souls. This is much like the way a person chooses a profession in our world—according to personal character and the inclination of his or her heart.

Our pace of progress depends on our own will, how much we desire to know what is written in the books and our desire to know the upper world. The study makes a person begin to prefer the nearness of the upper world and to choose living according to spiritual laws rather than living according to the corporeal laws of our world. A person necessarily connects him- or herself to good, positive forces through this study.

We will always believe, and hang our hopes, on a change that will come from above, on a change of luck, on things getting better. It is true that what happens in our world today is a direct consequence of what comes down to us from the upper spiritual world. But we can make sure that only good forces descend on us and give us bounty, provided we know how to act in the spiritual worlds.

We will know how to act correctly by a practical and systematic study of the structure of the upper worlds. We will learn to avoid a negative reaction to our actions, to do only things that will provoke a positive change in our lives. If our connection with the upper worlds were organized correctly, it would be for the best of all of us, for our own people, for the other nations, and for the whole world.

SCIENCE, TECHNOLOGY, AND HUMAN NATURE

An overview of the state of humanity in our time yields a sullen picture, one that could aptly be named "a crisis."[1] It seems that in all areas of life—personal, familial, national, and international—we are faced with escalating situations to which there are no solutions in sight.

Depression is soaring,[2] followed by an increasing escape to drugs[3] and alcohol. The family unit is disintegrating; domestic violence, alienation, and divorce are perpetually increasing; social polarization widens; and corruption in the government has become daily news. War and terrorism have become globally commonplace; social decline, natural disasters—all those and more have become a daily reality to many.

Thus, uncertainty and insecurity increase. While past leaders could make long-term plans for humankind and determine their short-term actions accordingly, today they cannot outline clear policies for the continuation of our existence.

In and of themselves, crises are not negative. Humanity has been in crises before; and every time they have produced more highly evolved states. A crisis in one field leads to the rising of new fields. But today the situation seems essentially different: collapse is happening in almost every field of life and almost simultaneously.

This escalating crisis is even more perplexing in view of the achievements of science and technology, which have provided us the means to make our lives much more comfortable and easier than ever before. It seems that time and space have shrunk and that the world is truly becoming a small village.

Theoretically, science should have provided us a sheltered world, one where we could live peacefully and safely without a care in the world. Many thinkers, supporting modernization, were certain that industrialization and progress would place humanity on the brink of a secure and bountiful era.

If humankind had only wanted, the existential hardships of many could vanish. We could provide for the entire world and make certain that no person would be troubled struggling for survival. In such a utopia, we would establish world peace and bring the whole of humankind to prosperity and affluence.

Regrettably, this is not the case, in part because of how we use our knowledge. Since ancient times, sages withheld knowledge from unworthy people. They feared that people would abuse the knowledge of natural forces. The knowledge in itself is not harmful, but is often used detrimentally because the fundamental priority of human nature is to use knowledge for egoistic purposes. This approach compelled sages to be very cautious when accepting disciples, since, as possessors of this knowledge, the responsibility for conveying it lay on their shoulders.

In time, those in possession of this knowledge began to deteriorate as well. They started to sell the wisdom in return for the satisfaction of their material desires for honor and power. The increasing material temptations prompted the ancient sages to relinquish settling for mere sustenance while turning their entire efforts to research Creation. As their egos grew, they began to crave both research and material pleasures.[4] This decline of the sages allowed the knowledge to be disseminated among undeveloped people who wished only to satisfy their desires for money, power, and domination.

Although this process has continued throughout history, the Renaissance and the industrial revolution mark a turning point where manifestations of an increasing egoism grew bodacious. Since that time, the picture has greatly worsened. Today the arms industry has become one of the leading industries in the world, and firearms have become weapons of mass destruction.

Alongside the advancement of science and technology, there exists an inner growth within each person and in humankind as a whole. Nature pushes us to use everything around us for personal gain, even if we are unaware of it. In fact, it is the growing egoistic search for self-fulfillment at the expense of others that causes us to misuse the achievements of science and technology.

There is a dichotomy between the advancement of knowledge and the moral standard of the people using it. While we acquire more and more knowledge and consequently ever greater power, the natural development of the ego leads directly to moral decline. In light of the above, the ancient sages' inclination to conceal the knowledge from the people becomes obvious; these conditions and the limitations were only placed for our own well-being.[5]

We therefore see that human nature and its inherent egoism is the reason for the polarity between scientific evolution and personal and collective happiness. The intensification of the ego is the root of escalating personal and global crises. Thus, knowledge and progress will not help humanity, only bring it to an extreme where both evils (the growth of the ego to a colossal magnitude and the accessibility of weapons of mass destruction) will unite.

Having realized the negative potential that it holds, it would be gross naïveté to condition humankind's well-being on further scientific advancement. Instead, we must turn all our energy to seek a way to mend humankind's nature.[6] It is safe to say that a breakthrough in this field is virtually humankind's only hope.

THE ORDER OF SOULS

In each generation over the past six thousand years, souls have descended that were here on previous occasions. None of us is a new soul; we have all accumulated experiences from previous lives in other incarnations.

Souls descend to earth in a special cyclical order. The number of souls is not infinite; they return again and again, progressing toward correction. The same souls are encased in a series of physical bodies that are more or less the same, but the types of souls that descend are different from one another. This is referred to nowadays as "reincarnation," but Kabbalists use the term "development of the generations."

This intertwining, the connection of the soul and body, assists in the correction of the soul. The human being is referred to as soul, not body. The body itself can be replaced, just as organs can now be replaced. The body is useful only in that it serves as an encasement through which the soul can work. Each generation physically resembles the previous one, but they are different from one another, because each time the souls descend they are imbued with the added experience of their previous lives here. They arrive with renewed strength obtained while they were in heaven.

Thus, each generation possesses different desires and goals from the previous one. This leads to the specific development of each generation. Even a generation that does not reach the desire to know the true reality or a God-like recognition accomplishes the task by the suffering it endures. That is its way of making progress toward the true reality.

All souls are derived from the soul of the first man, *Adam ha Rishon*. This does not refer to Adam as a mere personality from the Bible. It is a concept of spiritual, inner reality. Parts of the soul of the first human being descend into the world, taking the form of bodies, leading to a connection between body and soul. Reality is directed in such a manner that the souls descend and correct themselves. When they enter into a bodily form, they raise their level 620 times above the level from which they began. The order in which souls descend into this reality of wearing a body goes from light to heavy.

The soul of the first human comprises many parts and many desires, some light, others heavy, based on the amount of egoism and cruelty they possess. They come into our world, the lighter ones first, the heavier ones following. Accordingly, their requirements for *tikkun* (correction) differ.

In their descent into the world, souls have gathered experiences from their suffering. This is called the path of suffering, as these experiences develop the soul. Each time it is reincarnated, a soul has an increased unconscious urge to seek answers to questions about its existence, its roots, and the importance of life.

Accordingly, there are souls that are less developed, and souls that are more so. The latter have such an enormous urge to recognize the truth that they cannot limit themselves to the confines of this world. If they are given the right tools, the proper books and instruction, they will attain recognition of the spiritual world. Kabbalah also describes the descending souls as either pure or less refined. It is a measurement in direct proportion to how much the souls require correction. Souls requiring a greater correction are considered less refined.

As different souls descend, they require guidance unique to that specific generation. This is why in each generation there are people who lead us in our spiritual progress. They write books and form study groups to convey the method for discovering reality that is most suited to that generation. Before the soul of Ari appeared, there was an era of experience-gathering and perseverance in this world. The souls' existence was sufficient to make progress toward correction. The suffering they accumulated added urgency to their need to achieve correction. The desire to leave their suffering behind was the motivating force behind the development of the generations.

That era continued until the sixteenth century, when the Ari appeared and wrote that from his generation onward, men, women, and children in all the nations of the world could, and were required to, engage in Kabbalah. The time had arrived in the development of the generations in which souls descending into the world were able to recognize the true reality and were ready to complete their correction by the special method the Ari had developed. They could now achieve what was required of them.

Souls have but one desire while existing within physical bodies: to return to their roots, to the level they were at before their descent. Physical bodies, with their desire to receive, pull the souls back into this world. People consciously wish to rise spiritually. The great effort spent on the friction created by this dichotomy is what assists them in rising 620 times above their previous level. If a soul does not complete its task in one lifetime, the next time it descends into the world, it will reincarnate more deserving of correction.

Sometimes, we believe that we should deny our desires and longing so that in the next reincarnation we will be more successful. We think we should not desire anything except a little food and to lie idly in the sunlight, as would a cat. However, the contrary is true. In the next round, we will be even more cruel, demanding, exacting, and aggressive.

The Creator wants us to be filled with spiritual pleasure, to be complete. That is possible only through a great desire. Only with a corrected desire can we truly reach the spiritual world and become strong and active. If our desire is small, while it cannot do great harm, it also cannot do much good. Desire is called corrected only when it functions out of the proper influence. It does not exist in us automatically, but is acquired while studying Kabbalah in the correct manner.

THE PYRAMID OF DESIRES

A pyramid of souls exists, based on the desire to receive. At the base of the pyramid are many souls with small, earthly desires, looking for a comfortable life in an animal-like manner: their focus is food, sex, and sleep. The next layer comprises fewer souls, those with the urge to acquire wealth. These are people who are willing to invest their entire lives in making money and who sacrifice themselves for the sake of being rich. Next are those who will do anything to control others, to govern and reach positions of power. An even greater desire, felt by even fewer souls, is for knowledge; these are scientists and academics, people who spend their lives engaged in discovering something specific. They are interested in nothing but their all-important discovery. Located at the zenith of the pyramid is the strongest desire, developed by only a small number of souls, for the attainment of the spiritual world.

We all have this pyramid of desires within us, which we must turn upside-down so that the sheer weight of the top will compel us to aim for the purest desire, the infinite desire for truth. We must reject and discard all our earthly, egoistic desires and put every effort and energy into increasing the desire for spirituality. This is achieved through the proper way of studying.

When people truly wish to increase their longing for spirituality, then the light around them, the spiritual world hidden from them, starts to reflect back on them, making them long for it even more. At this stage, group study under a Kabbalist's guidance is crucial. A major change in the souls descending today is that they have a definite desire to achieve spirituality. Even ordinary people are seeking something spiritual, something beyond our world.

Although this "spirituality" may include all sorts of short-cuts, magic tricks, esoteric teachings, and groups promising answers to those who join them, nevertheless, it bespeaks the search for a different reality. If a generation displays a stronger desire within the souls themselves, a new method, suited to those souls, will emerge. In the last fifteen years there has been swift and active development in the descent of new souls. The desire of these souls is much stronger and more genuine than the desire of any previous generation. They are directed at achieving the real truth and nothing else.

When we truly comprehend how reality applies to us and how we are affected by it, we will cease doing that which is prohibited; we will insist on the right thing, and we will do it. Then we will discover harmony between the real world and ourselves.

In the meantime, we unconsciously err, and then realize we have erred. It may appear that no escape is possible. Humankind finds itself more and more in a blind alley, mired in increasingly difficult dilemmas. We will discover that there is no alternative to recognizing the spiritual world of which we are a part. This recognition will lead us to a new state of being in which we will consciously begin to act as one collective body and not just as individuals.

All people are connected to one another, from one generation of souls to the next. We all share a collective responsibility. That is why the Kabbalists are regarded as "founders of the world." They influence the entire world, and the world influences them.

THE REMEDY TO THE BOUNDARIES OF THE WILL TO RECEIVE

Our happiness or unhappiness is contingent upon the satisfaction of our desires. Satisfaction of desire is defined as pleasure and may appear in various forms. Fulfilling our desires requires effort. In that regard, Rabbi Yehuda Ashlag states the following: "It is well known to researchers of nature that one cannot perform even the slightest movement without motivation, meaning without somehow benefiting oneself. When, for example, one moves one's hand from the chair to the table it is because one thinks that by putting one's hand on the table one will thus receive greater pleasure. If one would not think so, one would leave one's hand on the chair for the rest of one's life."[7]

The intensity of the pleasure depends on the intensity of the desire, but as satisfaction increases, the desire decreases respectively, and in consequence, the pleasure too. If we look into our pleasures, any kind of pleasure, we will see that they all diminish as soon as fulfillment begins. The maximum pleasure is experienced with the first encounter between the desire and its fulfillment. For example, the greater the hunger, the greater the pleasure derived from its satisfaction. However, if we are given food when we are no longer hungry, we will be unable to feel any pleasure and will probably even feel repelled.

Thus, pleasure from something depends on the desire for that something; there is no pleasure in the desired thing itself. As the sensations of fulfillment and pleasure fade, we are prompted to pursue new pleasures.

Humanity normally deals with the problem of the dissatisfied will to receive in one of two ways: the first is acquiring habits, and the second is diminishing the will to receive. The first way relies on "taming" desires through conditioning. First, one is taught that every action yields a certain reward. After performing the required task, one is rewarded with the appreciation of teachers and the environment. Gradually, the rewards are withdrawn, but the person labels the act as rewarding. The performing itself yields pleasure, since "habit turns to second nature."[8] We feel satisfied when our execution of the act improves. The second way is primarily used by Eastern teachings and relies on diminishing the will to receive, since it is easier to not want than to want and not have.

At first glance, it seems that we have learned to efficiently use these two methods, as long as we continue to pursue the next pleasure and continue with our daily routine, hoping for the best. Though not obtaining the desired thing might inflict a sense of want or dissatisfaction, in many cases the very pursuit of fulfillment becomes a temporary substitute for the actual filling. When we search, we feel vital, since our desires and goals are renewed, and we have hope of obtaining fulfillment.

Yet the more the will to receive grows, the less applicable these substitutes become. The increasing egoism neither enables us to submit to religious and/or moral systems, nor permits us to silence it.

The fifth degree of the will to receive—the desire for spirituality—begins in disillusion. It results from our inability to satisfy ourselves. Sometimes we feel unable to satisfy our desires and remain empty, but more often than not, we seek comfort in knowing that this is how everyone lives, a sort of "sorrow shared is sorrow halved." When we can no longer satisfy ourselves, it is the beginning of the fifth degree in the evolution of the will to receive.

One of the ramifications of this pursuit of satisfaction and relief is the use of drugs and alcohol. Those are mostly used as means of distraction from the bleak reality, but the consequent addiction to them becomes a serious problem in and of itself. Extreme cases of disillusion end in increasing numbers of suicides.[9] In fact, depression and drugs can be described as modern-day maladies, and modern medicine is helpless when confronted with the roots of mental diseases such as depression.

Nevertheless, depression is only an expression of the newly evolving degree of the will to receive in humanity. This new desire demands fulfillment, though for the time being it is unclear what that fulfillment is and how to obtain it. Frustration caused by a sensation of emptiness compels humanity to run amok seeking fulfillment and is the root of the contemporary international crisis and worldwide terrorism.

We are standing on the threshold of yet another phase in the unfolding of the fifth degree of the will to receive. Until today, we have managed to cope, either by one of the above-mentioned ways or by escape to alcohol and drugs.

Though our current state may not be at its best, we tend to believe that relief will come if we only obtain one of the familiar pleasures: sex, money, honor, or knowledge. Yet, we will soon find out that we will have no more role models and no idols to look up to. We will be utterly disillusioned with our existence in the world and lose hope of ever finding peace of mind. Moreover, we will be convinced that even if we are reborn into completely different conditions, we will still find no rest.

Seeking to remedy our souls and trying to understand the meaning of suffering and the meaning of life, we are pushed beyond this world, beyond the boundaries of our reality that offers pleasures that do not fulfill this new, incomprehensible desire. In fact, the question we face pertains to our origin, our root, whether there is a guiding hand in our life, and if there is, whose is it and what does He or She want? It is only through the wisdom of Kabbalah that one may find the answers to these essential questions.

THE POWER IN THE BOOKS OF KABBALAH

Kabbalistic books are not like ordinary books we buy in a bookstore, or like the ones we study in university. They are not even like the ones we study from in *Yeshivot* (rabbinical colleges). The special thing about the genuine books of Kabbalah is that reading them improves the readers, makes them feel something new, and helps them to develop their sixth sense. It is with that sixth sense that a person begins to discover spirituality, to see what is beyond our world. With it, he or she begins to see the forces behind the objects of our world.

The minute we are able to go beyond this outer shell before us, we will begin to feel the forces that control our reality. Then we will be able to connect with those forces, influence them, see what exactly we are doing right and what we're doing wrong. With this understanding in hand, we will discover how we should behave in order to match ourselves with a supreme and mighty force that surrounds the entire reality. This way we will be able to live consciously in a better world for all of us.

I do not mean to say that Kabbalah teaches us how to improve our lives at the expense of others. On the contrary: the contact with the upper world teaches us how to refrain from hurting others, how to attain the true desire to give. The laws of the upper worlds are the only laws that exist in reality; they raise humanity to the spiritual degree of Man. We currently have no contact with them, and because of that we break them and thus inflict harm on others and ourselves.

The Upper Will, another name for the Creator, wants us to be His partners. He sees us as His children, as all the books say. What we call "the end of correction" and the "coming of the Messiah" is really an ascent of humanity to the degree of the Creator, where we unite. People become united with the Creator according to their individual awareness and the strength that they request from above and receive or acquire. Then they begin to be a part of the global spirituality. Only in this way can a person avoid trouble in this life, because all the troubles come for the sole purpose of forcing us to search for the reason for them, and then one discovers that the reason for them is detachment from the upper spiritual worlds, from spirituality.

To begin achieving this level of awareness, I propose reading books, listening to cassettes, reading the texts on our Internet site (www.kabbalah.info), and studying the nature of our duty to the upper force. Most important, we have to start thinking and picturing in any way possible that, behind all the events that occur, there is one supreme force that is trying to awaken us to take the good path. It is turning us toward reality.

The wisdom of Kabbalah is not just knowledge, but the wisdom of truth; it is a real science, a way to study the upper world and use it practically. The wisdom of Kabbalah provides us with an accurate method to enjoy the upper world, and it is the most practical way to learn how we can enjoy the entire reality correctly.

Unfortunately, most people do not understand that we can only change our reality with the united force of everyone together, by combining the power of will and the power of thought of the entire world. If all of us, as a people, relate differently to the force that comes from above, that will be the best way for us to influence reality and change it. Our souls have the powers of thought and desire, which, if used correctly, can induce an immediate change in reality. The collective power of our thought, if changed to appreciate spirituality instead of corporeality, will change the entire reality from above in our favor. This entire change depends only on how we relate to the mission at hand, against what has been placed before us from above.

We currently don't know the powers of thought and will that are concealed in us, though they are the greatest powers in the world. But if we shift our focus to spirituality and to the upper worlds, to what we call the guidance of the Creator, we will see that He, and only He, watches over everything that happens to us. We will begin to relate to it differently, start to learn how we can change those things, and take the leadership into our own hands.

There is no need to know how to change the situation right now. But the very desire and the effort to understand what is happening to us and who operates our reality and why, and the feeling that we are being perpetually lead from above toward some unknown goal, are by themselves enough to change our situation drastically.

KABBALAH AS A DAILY REALITY

At the end of his *Introduction to the Zohar*, Baal HaSulam writes that if we preferred spirituality to corporeality and spiritual laws to corporeal laws, if we chose a spiritual leadership over the corporeal one, we would organize our world correctly, exactly like the spiritual world, and then our inner values would not collide with the values that come down to us, and we would feel pleasure and peace instead of pain and suffering.

When tragic things happen to us in this world, there is nothing we can do to change it. Things happen as inevitable consequences of earlier thoughts, and there is no way to act in the spirit against something that already descends on you from above. All you can do in this world is to try as much as you can to avoid bodily harm, in our world of consequences. If you really want to influence your reality to avoid future tragedies, you should rise upward, to your origin, your root, and the place where the root of your enemy lies as well, and begin to sort things out there. The immediate result will be that everything in our world will change, because there is nothing in our world that is not a result of the world above.

In many Jewish homes there are copies of the Zohar, mezuzahs (a text from the Bible that Jews place on doorposts), and charms. People think that there is some power in them, but in fact they do not help us today. We've come to a point in history when we have to rise above these things; we should go beyond them and get to know the power itself, its operations on us, rather than thinking that if we put up a mezuzah everything is going to be all right. We have to start being practical and focus on the upper force.

STUDYING KABBALAH

Before we study the Zohar, we must first study several introductory books. There is much to read and learn to know how to open the book and what to search for in it.

The Zohar is written for people who are already in the spiritual world. For those people this book is a guide as all holy books are, showing us exactly what needs to be changed in the upper world and the spiritual force to induce a change and correction of the situation in our world.

However, there are unfamiliar names and terms in the Zohar that confuse new readers and potentially alienate them. Although these words are closely related to your life, right now you don't feel the connection, because you still don't feel that you are inside all these worlds. If you begin to study this wisdom, you will begin to feel them and see them. Today every person is capable and worthy of seeing and feeling the higher spiritual worlds through this world.

By studying about the upper worlds, you become connected to them and begin to experience the entire reality in a way that makes you see how it is possible to live without a body, only with our souls. You will see how souls descend to this world and become clothed in bodies, how our future is determined, what the past was, and what is the reason for everything. This way you will be able to know all the reasons and the consequences, and you'll know how to relate to your future and correct it.

It is impossible to get to this stage without knowing the upper world. The Creator wants us to live in all the worlds, and He is already forcing us to begin the study of the upper worlds quite unpleasantly. We must take into account that the situation will not get any easier, but only harder. We have been given the land of Israel, but now it is time to start learning how to live there in order to obtain the spiritual power concealed in it. Only then will we be able to build the Temple in the heart of each and every one of us.

A SPIRITUAL TASK

Reality can be changed by anyone, so long as he or she is thinking of the Creator. If his or her soul has ripened through all the cycles and its time has come to know spirituality, it is inevitable that he or she will have to enter the process of spiritual correction and learn to manipulate the spiritual powers. It doesn't matter where we are in the world, there will be torments and catastrophes standing ready for us wherever we go, as long as we do not realize it. In the end, we are at the center of the world, and there is no escape from that.

I anticipate that if we do not wake up now, there will be an increase in our troubles. The more we neglect the matter, the stronger will be the force that we will need to put us back on track. It is just like physics: when you throw something and it is diverted from the right path, the longer it continues off track, the greater its deflection and the greater the force needed to bring it back to the right track. That pattern will happen with us, too, if we do not change our ways. We don't have a choice but to start listening to what is happening with us.

It is most urgent to realize that nothing happens without a good reason, and that our behavior influences what comes down to us from the upper worlds. We cannot act like small children, crying and searching for ways to escape the troubles of life. We must become part of a mature humanity: one that knows what it is doing and can assume responsibility for its actions. This change in attitude will begin by keeping in mind that there is always a reason for our condition. That realization will prompt a larger shift in our consciousness, and then we will start to look for the reasons behind everything that happens to us in this world.

This awareness is inevitable for everyone in our generation; however, those people whose souls are not yet ready can live anywhere they choose and be completely unaware of what is happening. Those who are ready will face many obstacles until they begin to use the upper force and implement their assignment of correction. These troubles will not leave them until they start taking the right path. Everything comes from the upper force which operates on souls and pushes them according to their own pace of development, and those whose time has come to know the upper world simply cannot escape.

As I have said before, the world is built like a pyramid. Souls develop slowly. Some are beginning the process right now, and some still wait in line. I do not expect everyone to rush off seeking what the Zohar speaks of, but for those who do have the feeling that it belongs to them, that mission rests on their shoulders. People who ask the question "What is the meaning of my life?" are ready to know the spiritual world. This question comes from above, and there is only one answer to it: know the force that awakened the question to begin with, bond with Him, approach Him and work alongside Him.

HOW TO STUDY CORRECTLY

If an ordinary person were to begin studying a Kabbalah book in the right way, meaning after having studied the introductions and gone through some preparations, after being given a certain "key," he or she would see how to communicate with the forces that act on our entire world and would know what to do with them.

In a Kabbalistic prayer book it says, for example, "Extend light from *Partzuf Leah,* pass it through *Partzuf Zeir Anpin* to its three *Sefirot* of *NHY,* then come down to *Rachel,* then couple them one with the other." This is the sort of material you will find in a Kabbalistic prayer book, which is in essence a manual with exact instructions about how to change things in the control room of reality and what to change above to induce the desired change below. But without sufficient preparation, it makes no sense and would not lead the reader to any further understanding.

In all previous generations, the Creator raised a few souls to do their work for the collective, but in our generation, everyone must do this work according to his or her own ripeness. Everyone must open the books of Kabbalah and begin to study the instructions to learn how to change reality. We have to reach the same level and quality of performance within ourselves as is described in the books to make the necessary changes in the upper worlds. All of humankind will eventually have to enter that control room and everyone will come to a place reserved for him or her alone.

The prayer cited earlier describes the way desires and thoughts about reality are meant to be used. The only force that can influence reality is the power of thought and humankind's willpower. Kabbalists have prepared these prayer books as manuals that show us how to work with our desires. We only need to know how to read them and learn what to do, and we are required to do that right now.

The Creator wants us to manage reality by ourselves, seemingly without Him. By studying the books we become able to perform the things that are written there. We attain His degree and become His partners in every way, obtaining things that are hard for us to describe: wholeness, spirituality, pleasure, tranquility, the feeling of endlessness—eternity above and beyond life and death. There are no words to describe those feelings. Only those who experience that can see the difference between this reality and our world.

But I am talking only about what we must do. I am not talking about what we will attain; things that go beyond this world—unimaginable pleasures, splendid attainments that give you anything you might wish for.

There are two ways to teach a person to do his or her work. The first is short, fast, and painless: it is called "the path of Kabbalah." The second, however, is a way of continuous torment and pain called "the path of pain." Right now, we are advancing through pain, and to prevent a major catastrophe from inflicting horrendous pains on all of us, we must turn to these books and work on how to study them to begin changing the world.

The upper power works on us slowly, over years, but every now and again, when some time has passed and we have not made sufficient progress, that power intensifies and begins to move in a crooked way instead of directly. We can clearly see this process in our past: think about how much humanity has gone through in the past two thousand years compared to what it has gone through in the last one hundred years. This pace will only quicken: in one year we will experience the equivalent of several years in the past. Each year the pace will increase and become more intense, making it ever more crucial to change the world for the better. We must hurry and fulfill our mission and not wait for the terrible blows that will eventually make us do it anyhow.

Reality already exists. It is up to us to make it materialize for better or for worse. Kabbalists cannot change the situation by themselves. They need a group of people with whom to study and help them try to change things. But today, even that is not enough; we now need the entire Jewish people, or at least the majority of them, to understand their mission and begin to advance in spirituality and study the structure of the upper worlds.

THE QUESTION OF ISRAEL

The awakening desire for spirituality is called "the land of Israel." The people who lived in the land of Israel before the ruin of the Second Temple were in spiritual attainment. This means that the spiritual degree of the people of Israel and its presence in the corporeal land of Israel matched at that time. In that state, the people merited living in the land of Israel. When the people of Israel lost their spiritual degree and yielded to egoistic desires—due to the growth of the ego—the mismatch between their spiritual level and their presence in the land of Israel prompted the ruin of the Temple and the exile.

While the past spiritual fall caused the exile of the people of Israel from their land and their dispersion among the nations, today the situation is reversed: the physical return to the land of Israel preceded the spiritual return. Nevertheless, the match between the spiritual root and the corporeal branch must be kept, and for that reason the people of Israel are obliged to attain the spiritual degree called "land of Israel." For that objective, the wisdom of Kabbalah is a means for the people to correct themselves.

When Rabbi Ashlag completed his *Sulam* commentary on the *Zohar,* he wrote, "From these words we learn that our generation is the generation of the days of the Messiah, hence we have been awarded the redemption of our Holy Land.... We have also been awarded the revelation of the *Book of Zohar* ... but in both, we have only been awarded a gift from the Creator, but we have not received anything in our own hands."[10]

The physical end of the exile and the return of the people of Israel to their land is not enough. A spiritual return is required. Baal HaSulam distinguishes between what he calls "a time of giving" and "a time of receiving." A time of giving pertains to the creation of potential existence by the upper force; and the time of receiving is the actual realization of the possibility.

Until the people are corrected, they will not feel comfortable in this land. That is why so many people leave Israel. "Not only are people in the Diaspora not enthusiastic about coming here to enjoy the redemption, a large portion of those already redeemed and dwelling among us are anxiously wishing to be rid of this redemption and return to their lands in the Diaspora."[11]

The uncertainty and insecurity of day-to-day existence in Israel is there to prompt its dwellers to rise to the spiritual level called "the land of Israel." The goal of the upper force is to bring humankind to search for the reason, the root of all processes. All the pressures on the nation of Israel by other countries, and its interior social, personal, and national level crises, exist only to compel people to ask about the purpose of their existence in this world.

Some people contend that if the entire Jewish nation were to come live in the contemporary state of Israel, the desired changes in the world would come about as a result. This is not true. Israel will become important, and people will go to live there only if we tell ourselves and the rest of the world that the country is important for everyone and that we are assuming our mission as the chosen people: to start building the spiritual center of the world there, which is what the world expects us to do.

We must work to attain the upper spiritual worlds everywhere on the planet, but especially in the land of Israel. Every place on earth has a different force acting on it. When a person moves from one place to another, certain forces are acting upon him that cause him to move. We cannot grasp how much we are operated like marionettes and have nothing of our own except the thought about the upper force and the desire for connection with Him. All other things in us are only operations from above.

Israel has a special force to it. If we live there, we must be in unique balance with the upper force; otherwise we will have to be expelled from the land as we were exiled before. But the four exiles have already passed, and there will not be another exile because the inner structure of the soul does not require it. Instead, torments will increase in Israel until we realize that we must ascend in the spirit to attain the spiritual land of Israel as well.

After the correction of all the attributes, both Israel and the other nations of the world will come together and unite, and we will feel the Creator completely. Until we attain that situation, however, the correction lies on the shoulders of the people of Israel, the representatives of the spiritual Israel in this world. The people of Israel should correct themselves before anyone else. Thus, to the extent that we correct ourselves, we will also promote the nations of the world toward their own correction.

If everyone in Israel would face his or her inner enemies, the external enemies would disappear; the inside creates the outside. The outside depends entirely on the inside, just as the lower degree depends on the upper degree. The lower degree is created by the Upper One and receives its sustenance from it. By the same token, the behavior of the nations of the world is a consequence of our own behavior.

According to what we learn from the writings of Baal HaSulam, masses of people should participate in advancing toward the end of correction. He speaks of a process of mass-correction of souls. In any case, one's private spiritual progress is different than that of the collective. For the individual, the correction is performed through personal ascents and descents, whereas for the collective, it is done by connecting with the leading individual. The nations of the world feel the delay in their progress; they feel dependent on Israel, but they only need Israel for the first corrections. Afterward, they will rely on themselves for their own corrections.

Today, the task of Kabbalists is to try to circulate the need for correction to the entire Israeli nation and to create a suitable method for everyone by publishing books and qualifying teachers. A lot needs to be corrected, but even a single shred of a thought creates immense positive changes and prevents terrible pains.

KABBALAH TODAY

Throughout history, during those times when Kabbalah was concealed from most people, rivulets of the wisdom still seeped through, which gave rise to various erroneous conjectures about its purpose. Even today, most prevalent concepts about Kabbalah are fundamentally wrong. Kabbalah engages neither in improving the human existence in this world, nor in mystical or ecstatic experiences.

The sole purpose of the wisdom of Kabbalah is realizing the desire for spirituality, which in turn leads a person to realize his or her purpose in life. Once that desire surfaces, a person begins to need the Kabbalah; before that, it is redundant.

In previous generations, when the desire for spirituality had not yet ripened, Kabbalists set up boundaries on the study of Kabbalah, aiming to filter out those with unripe desires. The few whose desire had ripened in them were imparted the method, despite all the limitations. Now that humanity is experiencing the surfacing of the last degree of the will to receive—the desire for spirituality—concealing the Kabbalah is no longer pertinent. The ban on studying it has been lifted and the filtering at the gate of the study is performed in an entirely different way: Being a method to acquire genuine spirituality, the Kabbalah naturally filters out those with other desires, such as for sex, money, or power. It simply cannot assist in fulfilling those desires.

For us to reach our true purpose in life, we must experience all the evolutionary phases along the way, starting with the first phase of the growth of the will to receive—the egoism—until we reach the fifth and last degree—the desire for spirituality. At the end of that state, a feeling of crisis and disillusion from this world awaits us. Only after using up all the desires of this world to the fullest, and still wanting, are we ready to discover the next degree of evolution: spirituality.

Exposing the wisdom of Kabbalah before the surfacing of the full power of the egoism would have resulted in a world filled with misconceptions about the connection between spirituality and corporeality, much more than it is today, deviating humanity from the correct evolutionary path.

Today, various establishments promise improved quality of life, a "quick fix" for our mishaps. However, even when they apply the name Kabbalah to their practice, they infuse it with alien and irrelevant substances. The current thriving of this industry around the Kabbalah results from a common subconscious sensation that the answer to the growing disillusion with life lies in the Kabbalah. This is yet another phase in the disenchantment of humankind from its attempt to satisfy the inflating ego.

We must understand that there is no one person who is artificially promoting the disclosure and expansion of the Kabbalah. The general law of evolution—aspiring to bring the entire creation to its purpose—is the force behind the current exposure of the Kabbalah. Thus, the wisdom of Kabbalah is breaking out from the caves into the center stage of human consciousness to finally correct humanity's egoistic nature, the very nature that has turned every human achievement into a menace.

5

FREEDOM OF CHOICE

In our world, we are almost completely dependent on nature's providence. We are compelled to be born; we do not choose our time of birth or our family, our talents, or the people we meet in this life. We enter an environment we never chose.

All my characteristics are predefined: the feelings, the aspirations, and the character. Everyone is born with his or her own *mazal* (luck). Moreover, it is said that "there is not a blade of grass below [in our world] that has not an angel above [a force from the upper world] that strikes it and tells it: Grow!" So is there any freedom at all?

Both nature and society evolve according to their own laws, and so do all the changes in the universe and the ever-greater catastrophes that happen, hence there is nothing that depends on us. But if everything in humankind is dictated from above, not only our characteristics and inheritance, but everything outside us, including the forces that lead us to the end of correction, to a predetermined state, what kind of freedom can we talk about or even think about?

On the other hand, if we just obey nature's orders, it is unclear why we were created in the first place, not to mention everything else around us. If everything is predefined and there is no freedom of choice, there seems to be no point to the whole of creation. The goal of creation, however, is not that everything will continue the way it has so far advanced, without any reason, but rather to attain completeness, precisely through our gift of free choice. For that reason it is vitally important that we find where and in what our free choice manifests.

No plant, animal, or person can tolerate the denial of their freedom. Despite our awareness of the rigid frameworks in our world, the aspiration for independence dictates our life. Animals that lose their freedom lose their livelihood and become weak. Nature will not tolerate any kind of slavery; all living creatures want to be free. Therefore, it is not a coincidence that in recent centuries so much blood has been shed just to attain a certain amount of freedom.

It sometimes seems that we must ignore the question about our freedom of choice and choose only the most convenient options. This is one of the most fundamental dilemmas in our lives. We must clearly see where we have freedom to choose and where we do not—what is up to us to decide and what is dictated from above. The problem is that in our current level of development, we can't see the limitations that are acting on us from above.

But if there are even one or two actions or decisions in our lives where we are free to choose, we must study and understand those things carefully, because they are the only means of expressing our freedom and changing anything in our fate. In all other things, we still remain under the laws of nature, the ones we can and the ones we cannot see.

RISING ABOVE NATURE

The human being is created in the image of the Creator. Therefore, knowingly or unknowingly, he or she aspires to have all the attributes that characterize the Creator. For example, the Creator is in a state of eternal and complete rest. Because of that we too aspire for rest, and all our movements are only a means to attain it. The Creator is one and unique, therefore, everyone declares how much he or she, meaning his or her ego, is also one and unique. Our aspiration to achieve things we think cannot be attained comes from our soul, which is a part of the Creator. We in fact aspire for the situation of the Creator, who is actually free. And this is the purpose of our existence. If that weren't possible, the concept of freedom would simply not exist.

Our freedom, our independence, is only possible to the extent that we are freed from our nature and can rise above it. That is because our nature is predetermined. To attain the real and absolute freedom, we have to activate a special mechanism to open the door of the cage of our corporeal world into a spiritual, eternal, and free realm.

We have to fight for our freedom. Our whole life is comprised of struggles for bits of fictitious freedom, which society obliges us to engage in. We try to be as it would have us be, and we are prepared to fill up our lives with empty acts, just to get some recognition and respect.

At first, we fight for freedom from the burdens of parents and the family. We try to escape circumstances that were forced upon us and the duties that make our lives difficult. We invest a great deal of effort just to attain this false sense of freedom. But to attain genuine freedom, freedom from our nature, where everything is predetermined, we have to make an effort. That freedom can be attained not in the afterlife, as religions promise us, but here in the corporeal world, in this very life. But for that we need to make an effort, to rise above our nature, "above our world."

"Above our world" means being in attributes of bestowal, which are above this world. Our world is all about reception, egoistic material, and a desire to enjoy. There cannot be any real freedom of choice in our current attributes, which are dictated from above. Everything is predetermined, except one thing!

Parents often move to a location where their children will receive the best possible education. They try to provide for their children an environment that will guarantee their children's good development, and they are absolutely right in doing so. Parents understand that when children are under the influence of a certain environment, there is no freedom of choice, and so parents will try to act in the one place where they can make a difference, the freedom to choose the environment that will provide positive influences for their children.

Kabbalah fully analyzes the influence of the environment on people. Its conclusions are unequivocal: people are absolutely dependent on their environment—willingly or unwillingly. Even when they object to it, and their whole lives are wasted rejecting and trying to get away from it, eventually they will surrender and come to live in it.

Although many people dream of it, only a few succeed in getting beyond the influence of the environment. Yet we try again and again, because it is the only thing we have—the freedom to choose the right society for us and for our children. That determines almost everything in our lives. It is important to understand how to build such an environment for ourselves and what we need it for.

Kabbalah opens before us a complete and honest picture of the upper management, which has been closed to us until now. We see by it that each and every one of us, the whole of humankind, will have to accept the purpose of creation and the purpose of our lives, whether through difficulties in this life, or in the next, or by our own free will.

CONTROLLING MY OWN DESTINY

People often ask if previous lives dictate our present lives. They do, of course, but don't forget that there are future lives as well, not just previous ones. Today, every person has a chance in this life to affect his or her future lives. Every one of us should know how to influence our lives correctly, how to study the laws by which the influence continues from life to life.

A person can pass on a lot of vital information from one life to the next, thus preparing for a better life in the next round. We can advance toward the purpose of creation within just a few lifetimes and accumulate our attainments. We are the only creatures in the whole of creation that are given that opportunity.

We can determine our own destiny and consciously influence the surrounding environment. Our whole world depends on the light that comes down to us and clothes everything around us. This invisible light revives the entire reality. People can control the descent of this light to our world. The acquisition of a spiritual screen through the study of the wisdom of Kabbalah enables a person to control the descending of this light. That person can open a Kabbalistic prayer book and act according to the orders that are written there, instead of waiting for heaven's mercy.

A man or woman who can follow these instructions feels the upper light pass through him or her and as a result feels confidence and the perfection of the attainment. He or she knows what is going to happen and how to control it. This is where the real freedom of choice appears. In this level of bestowal, a person has full control over his or her life, the future, and the whole of nature. He or she brings to our world all the goodness through the upper light, and that light reflects back doubled and tripled.

OUR SPIRITUAL COMPOSITION

The evolution of the generations in the world is nothing more than an appearance and disappearance of physical bodies. The souls, however, that fill the physical body, the primary "I," do not disappear. They only change the body that carries them. Therefore, all the generations, from the first to the very last, are considered to be one generation that has been stretched over thousands of years, from the cradle of humankind to its final correction and the attainment of complete rest and wholeness.

Because its substance comes from an upper level, the demise of the body makes no difference to the soul. Physical death is as meaningless to our soul as cutting our nails or our hair is to the physical body. Nails and hair belong to the vegetative part in us, whereas the physical body belongs to a higher degree, the animate level. By studying how the soul is dressed in the body, a person is freed from death in his or her life.

To understand what the upper force allows us to choose, what is left to our free will, we must first examine our "I," the four elements that comprise us. The first element is called the "bed," the foundation. It is the basic, primary substance of which we are all made. That is what we received from the Creator. It is what defines our essence. The Creator created it *ex nihilo,* out of nothingness, something new that did not exist before. This is the substance that is imprinted in every one of us and predetermined in advance.

The second element is made up of the laws of the evolution of our essence. These laws do not change; they are predefined by the Creator, because they extend from the nature of the essence and its predetermined form, which the essence strives to come to as the purpose of its creation. Every seed, animal, and human being has within it the program and the laws of its evolution, and we cannot influence it.

The other two elements, the third and the fourth, relate to our development, but they are external to the soul itself. Those are the external conditions that make voluntary changes in us, of our own free choice, but put pressures on us that we cannot control, sometimes against our will. Hence, the third element in our evolution is the external conditions that can partially change our path of evolution to the "right" way or the "wrong" way.

Take for example a seed of wheat. If we sow the same kind of wheat in two parts of a field and influence each part differently, such as blocking the sunlight on one side, not giving enough water, not weeding out the weeds, while the other side gets the best possible conditions, we will see how much external elements affect the growth process. Although we will get the same wheat from both sides of the field, the final quality of that wheat will depend on what difficulties it encountered during its growth.

The fourth element is changing the external conditions. We cannot directly affect ourselves, but if we provoke a change in our external conditions, we can determine our own future— our future thoughts, aspirations, and, in one word, the *quality* of our future.

The first element, the bed, and the second element, the laws by which our essence evolves, can be expressed negatively through inheritance: physical weakness, feeble-mindedness, or a psychological or spiritual weakness. Therefore, if one finds oneself the right place to develop, by going under a positive influence of society, he or she can attain wonderful results, much like the seed.

Only when we rise above nature both in mind and heart will we be able to observe it from a higher degree. For example, we can meticulously research the evolution of the wheat seed and influence both the course of its life and the number of lives it will have by putting it in the ground, and thus "killing" it, but also reviving it from its previous condition to a new life.

These processes can be done only with vegetative nature, because there are no cycles of life and death among inanimate objects. It is impossible to rise above our animal nature without help from above. Thus, we cannot investigate outside this nature with our ordinary senses; even the most sophisticated instruments cannot help us here because they were also built on the same level. Perceiving outside nature can only be done by means of attributes received from a higher degree.

We will be able to understand the nature of human life only if we rise above our level, which is the highest in our world, to an even higher level, the spiritual world. Once we reach that level, we will be able to research ourselves and influence our own lives, much like we research and influence the wheat. That is precisely what the wisdom of Kabbalah enables us to do.

If we compare our lives with the life cycle of the wheat we discover our own evolution mechanism. A seed that is put in the ground changes form completely until there is nothing physical left of it. It is turned to dust and becomes inanimate. But its new form emerges, and it takes on a new life. The former shape is completely gone and there is nothing left of it but the spirit, the force, the knowledge that instigates the appearance of a new life.

If we were in the degree of the vegetative, in the degree of the wheat, we would not be able to examine life and its transformations. We would not be able to see how the seed loses its former life and begins its growth again with all its former attributes passed on to the new life. Although nothing physical is left of the original seed, a new plant emerges from the former state; a new cycle of life evolves, a new entity with no recollection of the past.

OLD SOULS, NEW BODIES

What happens to our bodies after death is much like what happens to the wheat seed. The physical body disintegrates and we receive a new body. But the soul, the former spiritual potential, still remains in the form of a gene, potential information that transcends from one phase, from the old physical body to the next, through a physical detachment called "death."

As long as the body has not fully disintegrated, the next cycle cannot start. Only when it disintegrates does the new cycle of evolution begin. That is why Jews bury their dead without delay. There are even some practices that enable the new life to begin sooner, such as adding lime to the grave so that the body will rot faster—as though asking for the new phase of correction to begin sooner.

The transition from life to life requires a complete disintegration, just like the wheat seed, until only the essence remains: a pure power, denied of any physical clothing. This essence is called the *reshimo*. Between the degrees, between one life cycle and the next, there is a severance, a void. For this reason a person cannot see the transitions from phase to phase. However, a Kabbalist transcends from cycle to cycle thousands of times. He or she controls the transitions, and in each of them leaves behind a *reshimo*. A Kabbalist doesn't need to leave the physical body to begin a new life because he or she identifies with the soul, not with the body.

It is even possible to go from this life to the next without dying. For this breakthrough to happen, for the soul to jump over its current corporeal incarnation to instigate a new degree of development, a person has to detach from his or her body mentally or spiritually, like the Kabbalist. Thus that person experiences many cycles during his or her physical life. In one lifetime he or she can go the whole way from beginning to end, to the purpose of creation, to the starting point of the soul.

We will be able to see the changes that occur in us with our own eyes only if we go beyond the degree of our world and enter the spiritual world, much like a person in a state of clinical death, watching from the side as the doctors fight for his or her life. From the upper level we can see what happens to us, research and manage our own lives and control their quality.

This force that transcends from our past lives, from the previous body to the next life, is called the "bed." It is the force that carries on the spiritual information itself, the essence of our lives. If the seed was a seed of wheat, it continues to be a seed of wheat. A certain soul will remain the same soul, but it will be dressed in a different body.

The soul dresses in a body that is suited for the execution of the program inside it. The attributes of the soul and the corrections it must go through define the characteristics of the physical body that it creates around it. We determine our future situation through our spiritual attainments in this cycle, meaning what kind of body and what conditions we will have in the next life. It is all up to the *reshimo,* which creates around it a new body after the demise of the current one. All the data about the corrections that the soul still has to go through is found in the *reshimo.*

A person can still come back to this world, once his or her corporeal assignment is completed. That person appears when he or she is completely corrected and his or her soul descends only to help others. From the same *reshimot* (plural for *reshimo*) that create the human body extend all the differences between people: their characteristics, talents, and tendencies are all determined by the internal attributes of the soul, by its need to realize what it must do in this world.

We receive the first element—the bed, the essence, the spiritual object, our spiritual gene—directly from the Creator. Therefore, it is clearly impossible to influence it in any way. That element includes the origin of a person within it, his or her echelon of thought, and the state of mind of his or her ancestors as well as the knowledge they have acquired. Afterward this knowledge appears as tendencies, as physical and mental characteristics of the personality of which we are unaware. They can be imprinted in a person as belief or skepticism, materialism or spirituality, or perhaps shyness or extroversion. These attributes are like the wheat seed that loses its corporeal shape in the ground. They are given to us without a physical body to contain them, through natural inheritance, and because of that they sometimes appear in the opposite form.

THE LAW OF EQUIVALENCE OF ATTRIBUTES

We do not say anything new in Kabbalah that goes against human logic. All the laws of the natural sciences speak in one form or another about each part of creation striving for the center, for a physical-biological balance (whether an atom, a molecule, an inanimate object, or a living organism). This is the principle of every law of nature, and it is also the principle of Kabbalah, but Kabbalah relates those collective laws of creation to humanity.

The very fact that we are a part of nature necessitates us to be subordinate to it. It is not a question of will, and neither is our very existence in this world. Hence, if a person accepts the laws of nature and keeps them, he or she will feel good, and if not, the opposite.

The collective laws of nature bring us back to a state of balance called the "center of creation." The minute you begin to want to go back to that center, as the law that returns does, you will feel that you are stepping on a comfortable road, because you agree with the force and keep its laws. On the other hand, if you do not know that law and act according to your own understanding, you will be punished. That is the way nature works—anyone who breaks its laws is punished, including people, who are inseparable parts of nature.

We are the only creatures who regularly break the laws of nature because all other creatures work only according to their natural impulses. Those impulses also exist in us, but they are not enough for us to know how to behave in nature, and if we do not acquire this knowledge, we will simply become extinct.

For that reason, we must understand that the best thing for us is to go along with the purpose of nature, which is (by definition) to bring all levels of reality—the still, the vegetative, the animate and the speaking—to perfection.

We must strive to always keep in mind that everything that we feel comes to us for a reason from the upper force, from the collective laws of nature. Those laws bring balance and movement to the physical-biological level, as well as to the spiritual level.

This balance is the return to the center from which we came. Hence, the first condition for adhering to this law is to keep in mind the thought that everything we feel comes from one source only, from one center, in order to pull us to it. That law is called the "Law of Equivalence of Attributes" or the "Law of Equivalence of Form."

The Creator's will is to bring us to perfection. I too seek to attain perfection, but for that, I need to study the program by which the Creator promotes me. If I want to know the Creator, the system (which works to benefit us) will appear before me. Baal HaSulam writes that in the beginning, one must understand that one is dependent on the Creator alone and that if one does not make contact with Him, one's life might become extinct.

Having thoughts about drawing closer to the center, to the upper force, is far more efficient than any ordinary prayer, or act of will. If we want to intensify our thoughts, we must dedicate time to a principle called *Ein Od Milvado,* "There is none else besides Him," and study the system of the worlds. Doing this will bring the light inside us. Hence, it is crucial that we have a minimal contact with the principle of creation, with the Creator, and with the system that controls the worlds.

For a person who is already studying the Kabbalah, it doesn't matter which language, words, or sounds define the spiritual degrees or states, be they the language of the Bible, the Kabbalah, or Mitzvot (commandments). But the language is very important for a beginning student for it can confuse and inflict undesirable materialization of the text and cause the student to imagine corporeal objects. Hence, the language of the Kabbalah is a technical one, which modern people can understand, comprised of *sefirot,* systems of worlds, *partzufim, behinot,* and sketches. The Kabbalah teaches us that there is a system with subsystems within it that operate on us—our body and soul—and on the whole universe.

When people want permanent contact with the upper force, they develop a new sensory organ and through it slowly begin to feel their connection with it. That upper force tells us how our communication system is built, how it works around us in the greater reality, and how it aspires to bring us back to the center. It tells us how it runs through the entire world and through humanity. That system is what motivates us and the world around us. You can call it the Upper One or Creator; it makes no difference. If you feel the collective power of the world, you will be able to understand how to conduct yourself correctly.

THE PROGRAM OF THE SOUL

The soul is like a computer program. Before it dresses in substance, it is no more than a thought, an idea, a collection of connections between events in various situations. The system the Creator built is also like a computer program; the Creator is the program. If we study it, we will be able to organize the situations we face in the best possible way for ourselves and for society. That program is not detached from our thoughts, rather it is inside us. But it is a still an object in and of itself.

The program, the Creator, doesn't change, no matter how much we might like it to. But thoughts and prayers, meaning our desires, are what change us. The Creator is a desire: "The desire to delight (please) the creatures." As a result of past suffering, we become better suited for this program; we feel it is suitable for us, that it seems to treat us mercifully.

Kabbalah explains that the upper force, meaning the plan of the Creator, is complete, and it is only the vessels that change. Everything depends on the changes in the vessels, not on the light, because the light does not change.

The light behaves intransigently, mercilessly. That modus operandi cannot be changed, because the light extends and works on the entire creation from its origin, from the point of the "end of correction," the point where the creature is equal to the Creator. Hence, this condition and the operation of the light on us force us to reach the same situation. It is therefore obvious that if we do not aspire for the same thing, we find ourselves under the pressure of a vicious power that pushes toward the center.

The equivalence of form is tantamount to your consent with the plan. I compared the plan of the Creator to a computer program, because they are both unchangeable. You can scream at your computer all you want, but it will not answer you until you fix the problem yourself. So it is with humanity's relationship with the Creator: before we correct ourselves, we have no reason to expect creation to treat us benevolently.

We turn only to He who can change, and only when there is hope that He will change. But that is a common mistake made about the Creator. Malachi states very clearly: "I the Lord do not change" (3:6), and indeed you are the one changing,

although the Creator makes you think that it is He who changes
and not you.

We are unaware of how much our sensory system depends
on the emotions, on our vessels. The slightest change, and the
whole world immediately looks completely different. But after
a person crosses the barrier and feels the upper world, meaning
the Creator, he or she begins to advance in spiritual degrees and
feels that the Creator always changes with respect to him or her.

CONTACTING THE CREATOR

I want to teach you how to do whatever you want using a special program in your "computer." The system in this computer
is nature, but humanity is the only part in this system that actually operates, which is why it sometimes seems as though nature
is caged in a box, in a computer, and only we are outside. We
are the only ones who can work with this program—receive
data, affect that data, and get a response to our actions on the
screen. I want to teach you how to use this program, because I
too learned it from my teacher, and I am convinced how effective it is.

Kabbalists are the only ones who use and control this program, and they pass on the knowledge about the right approach
to nature and how to control it from generation to generation.
Their books describe how this world can be managed. This wisdom is called *Hochmat ha Nistar* (the wisdom of the hidden),
because only a worthy person can study it, and for the rest it
remains a secret. If a person does not correct his or her attributes as nature demands, he or she cannot understand that wisdom. Even in our present situation, we can begin to learn this
wisdom. And even if we use it egoistically for the time being, we
will improve our situation and our lives.

To make contact with the Creator, a contact that existed
between the Creator and the soul before it came down to the

corporeal world and clothed itself in a body, a system was made that slowly brings us from the farthest point from the Creator to the nearest point to Him, to complete equivalence of form with Him. This goal is programmed into our system, and the system leads the entire creation to this ultimate goal. The program is the general law, intended to bring everything to perfection—Israel first, and then all other nations, and after them, the animals, the plants, and the entire corporeal world.

The general law acts like the law of gravity in our world: the source, called "perfection," attracts the entire reality and all the creatures toward it, but it is we Jews who stand directly opposite it. We are the first to be attracted to it, and that is why we feel its intense power as pain. If we do not aspire to the center more than its pull on us, we will feel pain, according to the depth of the gap between our desire to approach the center and the intensity of the pulling force. If the desire to advance is stronger than the pulling force, we will feel complete and content. If we relate correctly to reality, we will begin to understand that everything we feel comes from the Creator to force us to connect with Him.

And then a person relates to the reason that makes him or her turn to the Creator as a consequence. We relate to our desires as actions of the Creator and in fact the only desire that originates outside the Creator is the decision to turn to Him. The contact with the Creator and turning to Him become a goal, instead of a means to attain something. The goal, therefore, is the Creator, not ourselves.

That means that I must return to the place from which I came before my soul came down to this world. I must connect with the Creator while in this world. If I want money or rain, it is called *Lo Lishma* (not for Her name), the degree of still. If, however, I ask of the Creator permission to approach Him, to attain Him, then my goal is not me, but Him, the Creator, as Psalms says: "For in Him (the Creator) doth our heart rejoice" (33:21). This is the real purpose of creation.

Even when a person asks for rainfall, there is still the upper force behind the plea. Although it is not aimed at the real goal, it is still a prayer to the Creator. Whether we like it or not, we are tied to the Creator like the umbilical cord that ties a fetus to its mother.

But a person who prays unconsciously does not prevent future pains, because the Creator sends us those pains so that we will understand that there is a reason for the pain, which cannot be overlooked; without those pains humankind will never attain the purpose of creation. It is crucial to understand that the suffering is purposeful, that it comes from the Creator for a certain purpose.

The advancement toward the Creator begins the minute a person prefers contact with the Creator to anything, good or bad, and seemingly neutralizes his or her desire for worldly pleasures, an act known in Kabbalah as *tzimtzum* (restriction). Once a person attains the ability to control him- or herself, he or she goes on to acquire the ability to enjoy for the Creator's sake and not for his or her own, something that goes completely against human nature.

A person who wants to draw near to the Creator does not regard Him as a mere source of pleasure for egoistic pleasure. The person accepts everything that happens in life lovingly. Even the bad sensations are regarded as signs that his or her vessel is not corrected, because that is the reason we feel everything that comes from the Creator as bad. The pains and the bad sensations disappear. At first we feel the pains as bad, but then they are viewed as vital for our spiritual progress.

THE SCIENCE OF KABBALAH

It all started with believing in supernatural powers. People believe that there are individuals who are imbued with supernatural powers who can influence others and foresee and control the future. Those people are willing to spend fortunes on healing, defense from the "evil eye," and fortunetelling. They believe that evil thoughts can harm another person and that the damage can be so great that it will be beyond repair and might haunt a person forever, causing damage in every aspect of life, including business and family.

When someone comes to me with a complaint about suffering from an "evil eye," that person is in fact trying to say that someone influenced him or her badly, meaning someone acted in a harmful way through the power of thought. That person also believes that I hold the power to neutralize that evil thought through my own power of thought. If this person asks to neutralize another person's thoughts, then he or she believes in the power of thought and that thoughts do in fact act and come true in our world.

The power of thought is the single most powerful force in reality. Our experience tells us that the more subtle and elusive a power is, the stronger and less limited it is. Today, there are even scientists that recognize this. Radio waves, magnetic and electric fields, radioactivity, and gravity are all examples of forces that we know of only by their actions and the phenomena they induce in our world. There are, however, forces such as the power of the thought whose actions we cannot even identify.

Kabbalah is not about ancient mysticism; it is the most contemporary science and the one that is the closest to us. It is a science of the twenty-first century that studies the forces we cannot see, forces that operate our world and affect every moment in our lives. It is the science that will change the future of each and every one of us in particular, and the whole of humankind in general. The special thing about this science is that the study itself forms the connection with those powers. A person changes his or her life by simply studying Kabbalah. He or she finds a connection with the upper power, with the one that brought him or her to our world and arranged all of life.

The power of Kabbalah has but one goal—to bring humanity in the quickest possible way to its peak, meaning the recognition of all the laws of the upper world, as well as the ability to operate them. For every person is meant to live in both worlds together: in the familiar physical world and in the spiritual world, which determines everything that happens here. Using this power, a person becomes like that force through the study of the Kabbalah and conducts his or her life accordingly.

THE ROLE OF THE JEWISH PEOPLE

Kabbalah is a practical, up-to-date science that answers everything a person looks for in life. It is time to reveal the secret wisdom to everyone. The Kabbalah is becoming a practical science that anyone can learn to apply and use for his or her own needs. That is what Kabbalists have always been writing, and that is what the book of Zohar says as well. Today, we are obliged to recognize the wisdom of the Kabbalah and study it to control reality by ourselves, according to its own instruction.

The Kabbalah is a wisdom meant to lead the entire reality, which is meant for all people, not only Jews. However, there is an order of development. We Jews, the "chosen people," have to be the first to get to know the forces that come from the upper world and use them correctly, in order to convey that knowledge to the rest of the world and thereby conduct the entire reality. That is the Kabbalistic definition of being chosen. We must be the first to study it and pass it on to the rest of humankind. The progress of the Jews determines the progress of all the others.

I did not invent these concepts. They are all written in all the books of Kabbalah. According to the plan of the upper world, all creatures without exception must rise from their present situation to a much higher degree, and that can be done only through the study of the upper force and the connection with it. We can change our lives while in this world. We can avoid unnecessary pains and attain happiness, wholeness, and eternity. Then, there won't be any difference between life and a physical death, for we will be living in both worlds at once.

We Jews have a unique role: we have to find the way to rise from the corporeal life to a higher degree, to the spiritual life, and we have to show the world how it is done. That is the only thing that we are chosen for. In the meantime, we are not carrying out our mission, and that is why we look so bad and unworthy in the eyes of the nations. Because we have special souls, we have to be the first to work on attaining that knowledge and accordingly do what we must. We have no advantage over anyone, but only in that we have to start studying about the upper worlds, about the force, which comes from the upper world, immerse ourselves in that work first, and pass it on to all the other nations. This is what all the books of the prophets and Kabbalah say.

What we know as the laws of Judaism are rules that were set by the greatest Kabbalists in every generation. They set them according to the needs of their time and the goal that they wanted to attain. The goal was to preserve the nation and the Jewish tradition in order to cross all the exiles, until we come out of the last exile and return to the land of Israel. Their only goal was that we would not forget our Judaism and assimilate in the nations. That is why they set laws and customs that preserved what we had. It is a degree called "sacred still."

It is only thanks to those laws that we survived through this long exile and returned as Jews to the land of Israel. But since our return, our role as Jews has changed: the goal is now much more active. Baal HaSulam writes at the end of the introduction to the book of Zohar: "If Jews do not add the spiritual practice of precepts to the practical practice, meaning the study of the laws of the upper world and their utilization for man's development and his approach to the Creator, then we will no longer be able to exist."

The practical practice of Mitzvot, which had been so important during the two thousand years of exile, was the right thing to do. But now that we've been given the land of Israel again, and since we've begun to settle in it, we have begun a new era. We have to equalize our corporeal life with the spiritual laws of the land of Israel. What we refer to as the corporeal land of Israel is in fact a spiritual, sublime value with a great spiritual strength that can only be attained there.

If we continue to behave as we did in exile, we will not be able to go on living in Israel. We will not be thrown out of there, but the assignment of the chosen people will be forced on us mercilessly and ruthlessly. The upper force is guiding us to its one goal in the shortest and quickest way.

The Zohar promises that we are already in the last phase, and after that everything will fall into place. But there is a tough time ahead of us, called the "coming of the Messiah." During that time we must discover the upper laws, whose essence is bestowal and love of humankind, in order to learn how to use them for self-correction. This inner process of humanity's correction must be realized first in the Jews and in the corporeal land of Israel, and afterward in the whole of humankind. This is the ultimate way to manifest our freedom of choice.

6

THE PATH OF CORRECTION

The structure of creation is a lot simpler than we think: Everything happens within one's soul. The soul feels within it the Creator, itself, and the connection between them.

The soul is the only thing that was ever created, and it is all that exists besides the Creator. That soul doesn't feel anything outside itself and is only aware of its inner world. It is called *Adam* or *Adam ha Rishon* (first man), and it is divided into many parts. Each part is an organ of the body of the first man. The soul is, in fact, the very same will to receive delight and pleasure. Its parts, called "unique souls," are desires for reception of pleasure.

Each soul contains the 613 desires that the collective soul of the first man had before it sinned and broke into many pieces. In Kabbalah, a sin means receiving pleasure for our own delight, as opposed to receiving to bring contentment to the Creator. That was also the sin of *Adam ha Rishon*. As a result of his sin, his soul was divided into 600,000 separate parts, which came to be 600,000 individual souls. Each of these 600,000 souls consisted of 613 parts, also called desires. Those desires fell 125 degrees down from their original status, called the "root of the soul." The last degree to which they fell is called "this world," and it is the lowest spiritual degree of the soul. From that low state a person must correct his or her soul until it returns to its highest state, to the root of the soul. It must rise through the 125 degrees by a gradual correction of the 613 desires.

Adam's sin is misunderstood by us, as is the case with all the terms that take on a physical meaning in our world. Although the Torah seems to use the language of people, it really speaks of a different matter altogether, not about the issues between people. That is why there are misconceptions in the interpretation of the term *sin*.

The sin of the first man designates a descent from a spiritual height to the lowest possible degree, so that humanity will be able to start rising to the Creator of its own accord, consciously and out of its own free choice.

If we had remained in the state of sensation of the Creator in the upper world, where we were created, we would have had no way of acting independently and would have been under the control of the light like a robot, like a person under the shadow of a great personality. We would have had no freedom of choice and would be completely subject to the influence of the Creator. Hence, only when the Creator detaches Himself completely from humanity, hiding behind every veil, behind all the concealments that separate our world from the spiritual one, do we have real freedom of choice.

That fall from the spiritual world is called "the sin of Adam," although we now see how compulsory it was.

THE LAWS OF CORRECTION

The structure of creation consists of 613 laws. Each law is a system of correction that applies to each one of the soul's 613 desires. Some of these laws belong to the management of creation in general, and some belong to the individual system of providence in each and every creature. But without exception, they all operate within the soul, because besides the Creator, the soul is in itself the entire system of creation and reality.

The more one learns about these laws and begins to spiritually execute them, in their corrected form, the closer one comes to the degree of the Creator. That is to say, there is a ladder of 613 rungs that stands between our degree and the degree of the Creator. To climb a rung means to acquire a screen and yet another of the 613 desires of the soul.

After the sin, the vessel (the desire of the first man) kept breaking into smaller and smaller pieces. That is why the Torah speaks of the sin of Cain who killed Abel, which is in fact the next sin, the next breakdown in the vessels of the first man. To complete the correction of the soul, it is necessary to bring the souls further and further down, until they reach the level of our world. For the soul to begin to rise to the degree of the Creator independently, it must be completely detached from Him. It must drop below the degree of Cain and Abel, the generation of the Flood, the Tower of Babel, Sodom, and all the way down to the degree of our corporeal world.

We are at the very bottom of the ladder of degrees. When the soul descends to the degree of our world and is clothed in a body, it is completely detached from the Creator; it has no sensation of Him whatsoever, and then it thinks it is completely free. If we begin to rise from this situation, we will really be correcting everything as a result. That is why the uniform soul of the first man had to be broken: the souls needed to be brought down to the degree of this world to begin the process of rising up again.

ACTIVATING THE SPIRITUAL GENE

The entire plan of human development is imprinted in each person. It is the engine that pushes us forward and forces us to evolve. We have already succeeded in comprehending that the entire knowledge of the biological body can be obtained in our genes. But the plan for our spiritual development is also embedded in special genes, much deeper than our biological genes. These are our "spiritual genes."

From the moment a person comes into this world, this plan becomes operative and begins to control his or her life. It dictates a person's attributes, character, fate, and every movement. But it also allows a person the freedom to choose in many of the situations.

This plan exists not only in humans, but also in everything that exists in the universe, dictating the very process called "life." Unlike other parts of nature, that program is not inflexible in people, but evolves during their lives. The program is a series of consecutive data commands. Each commandment is called a *reshimo,* from the Hebrew word *roshem* (imprint). There is a chain of *reshimot* in each of us, from the moment we are born to the moment of our death, containing not only the information from our current life cycle, but from all the incarnations of our soul.

If we read the data in this chain of *reshimot* we will be able to go through all the stages of the development of the universe, as in a movie, from the earliest phases of the creation of the universe, the sun, and the stars, through the dinosaur era, and on to the farthest future. The collective law of the universe loses nothing but only changes from state to state.

If this chain of *reshimot* is our whole plan of operation, from the beginning of our life to its end, and if there is nothing that we can do but follow the written instructions, it would be interesting to know what is in store for us there, both as a whole and as individuals. But rather than find out the details of our destiny, it would be better to research the *reshimot* in the following manner: to learn what purpose nature sets for itself, what collective law the *reshimot* are supposed to bring us to, how we can study those *reshimot,* and then perhaps make changes, rebuild, and improve things.

The answer to that question can be found only if we dive into this plan of *reshimot* itself. When a person studies Kabbalah, he or she learns about that program and about those *reshimot,* but the contemporary person still has to make a certain effort to understand his or her life plan and to study the management system of the universe, so as to use it for the best.

Atzilut is the control panel and the source of light to our world. It determines the expansion of the light, which brings life, confidence, health, and peace to our world. The soul is in its most perfect state in the world of *Atzilut.* It is filled with eternal light and peace—equal to the Creator and filled with Him. From that state, the soul is "thrown" down to the lowest place called "this world." On its way from the world of *Atzilut* to our world, the soul gradually loses its light, and by the time it enters our world, it has lost all of it and remains with nothing more than reminiscences *(reshimot)* of its past. Those expansions are recorded in the *reshimot,* which afterward form the degrees of the ascent back from our world to the world of *Atzilut.*

The *reshimot* comprise two primary components: (1) a memory that remains from the light of the Creator that the soul was filled with before its descent to our world and (2) the power of the "aim for the Creator" (the desire to give), which held the soul in the uppermost spiritual degree. Those two components help us rebuild the spiritual sense, with which we can overcome the partition that separates the corporeal world from the spiritual world. That sense is something that the Kabbalists create within themselves. It is called a screen. The acquisition of a screen allows a person to control his or her destiny and improve his or her environment.

The descent of the soul from the upper world, where it is filled with light, to this world, where there is no light, is like a ball rolling down a staircase, hitting every step on its way down. Each bump is the *reshimo* that every person who studies Kabbalah learns to realize correctly, starting from the smallest *reshimo* created at the lowest spiritual step, down to the final and highest degree. Even in the first degree that a person attains, he or she rises from a state of unconsciousness to a state of higher awareness that awakens the desire for something sublime that can only be found outside his or her world.

THE ACCELERATION OF THE *RESHIMOT*

We were created in such a way that wherever we go, we look for pleasures and take every chance we can to satisfy our desires. Where do these desires come from, and how do we know how to satisfy them?

At any given moment there are new desires that awaken in us, at all levels of existence: on the physical, human, and spiritual levels. We don't feel all the physical desires, such as the desire of the cells to develop and the desire of the organs to act. Some of these desires are satisfied naturally, and some require our active participation to be satisfied. As a whole, the desires can be divided into three parts:

- Physical (beastly) desires, which exist in animals as well.

- Human desires, which exist only in human society, such as desires for wealth, honor, and knowledge, and human-spiritual desires, desires for something sublime that are clearly not of our world. Searching for supernatural phenomena, religious rituals, and Far Eastern techniques for the improvement of the body and the mind all express such desires.

- Spiritual desires, which aim directly at the unique Creator. The Kabbalah distinguishes the desire for the Creator from all other desires. Our desires for worldly pleasures are called "heart" while the desire for the Creator is called "the point in the heart."

The desires form in us as a result of the surfacing of the *reshimot,* the carriers of the information within us, forcing us to obey their demands. There is a chain of preliminary *reshimot* imprinted in us, which makes us aware of the desire that they awaken as they surface. We have no choice but to obey these desires, although we do not feel that there is something that we must obey—we simply want. It is as though the *reshimot* appear out of nowhere in the subconscious even before we detect them, and when they come into our awareness, we feel them as desires. There is only one thing that we want: pleasure.

The pleasure that the Creator wants to give to a creature is characterized by a single property: wholeness. He is unique and complete. There is none more complete than Him, and the purpose of the creature is to attain the perfection, the wholeness of the Creator.

Because the goal of the creature is to develop the point in the heart to the degree of the Creator, all our desires, the ones of this world (called "heart") and the ones for the Creator (called "point in the heart") must develop in both quality and quantity.

In every point in the heart there is a chain of *reshimot,* a stream of data and spiritual stages that the soul must go through to rise from the lowest situation to the highest—the degree of the Creator. Only after we attain the Creator from the opposite state, the lowest of all, is there a genuine desire (a vessel) for the sensation of tranquility, wholeness, uniqueness, and eternity. The point in the heart develops under the influence of the upper light. The point itself descended from the Creator. It is the only thing that we have from above that feels the Creator, whereas all other parts of us are made of a substance of this world.

Each new *reshimo* surfaces under the influence of the upper light on the point in the heart, just like plants grow under the influence of the sunlight. One begins to feel a new spiritual desire, which awakens the desire to satisfy and realize it. Thus, our entire life here is a realization of our *reshimot.*

The soul descends from the Creator, from the highest degree, to our world, the lowest degree, through the six thousand degrees of the worlds. As each degree is replaced with another, it leaves a *reshimo* in the soul, thus creating a chain of *reshimot* treasured in the heart. In the beginning, only the desires of the heart develop, desires for worldly pleasures—food, sex, family, wealth, power, knowledge, and so on. Then the point in the heart begins to develop, and a desire for something higher, undefined, suddenly emerges. A person begins to want to satisfy this desire, but cannot find the satisfaction anywhere. Then one slowly begins to realize that his or her corporeal desires are satisfied through the five natural senses. Each of these sense organs relay impulses of pleasure to our corporeal consciousness. But the new *reshimo,* the spiritual one, cannot be filled through these senses. It is not filled by worldly pleasures, but by the light. That is why the *reshimo* pushes us to attain the upper light, the Creator.

The nature of the light is to give. If the desire in the point in the heart will also be to give, then according to the intensity of this desire, the light can satisfy it. It is a necessary condition. The desire simply must resemble the light. Hence, a desire gets filled with pleasure only if it intends to give and not to receive. In other words, we can feel pleasure only if we give. The equivalence of attributes between the desire and the light brings us to the most complete nearness—adhesion—because the distance between desires is measured by the equivalence between them.

Until now we have only discussed the natural development of the *reshimot*. But the pace of the surfacing, realization, and development of the *reshimot* can be accelerated through the Kabbalah: studying from the right books, under the guidance of a genuine teacher, among a group of people who want to attain the purpose of creation.

Thus we see that we haven't any freedom of choice about the *reshimot*, the desires, the powers, and the mind. The only choice we have is whether or not to accelerate the development through the right external influence. The Creator influences us from within—through our character, the natural attributes, and the *reshimot*—and from the outside, through family and society. But He does leave us with one area of freedom: the environment. Through our environment, we can accelerate our development. We will evolve to attain the goal in any case, but we can accelerate the pace if we find other people to build a group and an environment with. Therefore, those who want to advance should aspire to gather in groups and at the same time become a part of a single group comprising of the whole of humankind.

It is impossible to skip any of the six thousand degrees of progress from below to above, by which the soul originally descended. It is impossible to skip any of the feelings and not experience them one at a time. All the situations must be experienced, but a society that aims at the right spiritual goal enables people to realize that their will to receive is bad and that they must get rid of it quickly. Thus, we become aware of our sensations faster. And that is our choice. Our desire to advance faster than the natural surfacing of the *reshimot* shifts us from the path of pain to the path of Kabbalah.

THE FREEDOM TO CHOOSE

As we discussed above, all throughout history philosophers have sought the answer to the question: "Is there freedom of choice?" They tried to define the concept of choice and reached the conclusion that only a limited freedom of choice in society is given to those who have a developed personality.

But among themselves, they understood that freedom of choice is always limited by our inability to control the future, because there is always the possibility that we could be run over by a truck, catch a fatal illness, or go into a coma. Of course, we can ignore such examples of the absence of freedom of choice, but that would not make life any easier. The evolution of genetics hasn't improved our situation either, but only strengthened the feeling that we are in a closed compartment, surrounded by chains of genes from which we can never escape.

And then comes the wisdom of Kabbalah, which Kabbalists regard as the last stage of the development of science, and we find that not only are we chained by our biological genes, but we are programmed throughout many lifetimes with a long and consistent chain of *reshimot* that is set in the mind, the heart, and the soul throughout all time, and that is what determines our lives.

By using our freedom of choice, we find that the self-acceleration of our progress brings us a wonderful outcome: If we want to realize our desires to attain the Creator by ourselves, we precede the pains and the natural pace of the surfacing of the *reshimot* and become free from the *reshimot* as though we escaped the pains.

And not only do we precede the surfacing of the *reshimot* and the pains, we become like a horse running faster than the flogging of the rider's whip. It is not that we awaken the *reshimot* before they awaken naturally in us, but we begin to be free of any outside pressure or influence. We act not under the influence of the *reshimot,* but out of our own free will. That is why they say that Israel is above the stars and fortunes. A person who advances independently toward the Creator, who is called Israel (*Yashar,* directly; *El,* creator), is not influenced by providence from above, for he or she leads the world independently, by preceding the instructions of the Creator.

Thus, by preceding the *reshimot*, we not only accelerate the process of advancement, we become leaders. When we precede providence, even before we know what it is and before the surfacing of the *reshimot*, we create the advancement and become completely independent and free. We feel ourselves above the entire universe, equal to the Creator.

INDEPENDENCE

The Creator created everything—worlds, *partzufim*, *sefirot*, and people—yet all those things are not regarded as creations. The term *creation* relates exclusively to something that begins to express an independent will. People who live in our world and perform actions are not regarded as creatures in the full sense of the word; only one who has an independent desire for the Creator can be called a creature.

A person who comes to study Kabbalah was brought to it from above. Only later, when the first independent desire for spirituality appears in that person, will he or she be called a "creature." That desire surfaces in us when we cross the barrier and stand at the lowest point in the spiritual world, called the conception of the soul. At this point a soul is called an "embryo" in a body of a spiritual *partzuf* called *ima* (mother). Kabbalists are regarded as creatures, each according to his or her own degree, because they possess such an independent desire.

People who do not possess that independent desire remain as "robots," messengers of the Creator. To them, there are no rewards or punishments, they haven't any choice, and they are led entirely by the Creator. The Creator gradually pushes them to accumulate pains that stem from their desire to enjoy only for themselves, from the egoism in which they were created. The experiences of pains they gather will force them to understand that egoism is bad and will prompt them to choose spirituality, with the help of the Creator.

The character has no bearing on the spiritual level of a person. Any act can be spiritual or egoistic, depending on the direction we give to our desires. What matters is not the act itself, but the intent that goes with it.

SOULS ON THE PATH OF PAIN

Every person was created with a complex corporeal body, and what one does in this world affects it. Therefore, what we do in our world is important. Whatever we do with an intention toward the Creator is considered a spiritual act, though the act itself might still be completely "beastly."

Nevertheless, anything we do inevitably leads us toward the purpose of creation. Even the pains we suffer in life do not come in vain, but are collected, and when the right time comes, they count in our favor. This happens slowly over many years, and we are not a consciously active part of it. To shorten this long path of pain, the Creator gave us the Torah, which directs us to the right goal less painfully.

Only in recent decades have a growing number of special souls begun to descend to our world, these souls having collected a sufficient amount of pain. These souls took the path of pain, accumulated deficits, and now those pains have turned into a yearning for the wisdom of Kabbalah. In future lives, these souls will delve into the study of Kabbalah more intensely and within a month or two attain fantastic results because they have accumulated a sufficient desire for it in their past lives. If a person has a strong enough desire to study and focuses just on Kabbalah for one purpose only, then in three to five years he or she will enter the spiritual world.

We pray involuntarily for what lies in our heart, since the desire in our heart *is* prayer. The role of prayer is to prepare our heart to yearn to feel the Creator. Therefore, a genuine prayer is called "the work of the heart"; the preparation is in our heart. Through a special kind of work, through study and examination, we can prepare ourselves to awaken the right desire.

We shouldn't have to refrain from pleasures, but whether we choose to receive them or not, the heart can't help but want them. It is impossible to impose anything on our heart. Only through vigorous work on ourselves, using a variety of means, will we be able to change the direction of the desires of the heart toward spirituality. Even in our current degree, we have to say that we "want to feel the Creator" even if it is for a mere personal pleasure. That desire must be complete because only then will it bear the desired result.

The Creator sends us mental and physical pains, and the only way that psychologists and doctors can ease our pains is to help people to communicate, cooperate, and support one another. Healing works because it helps to gather the souls into one collective soul.

Under no circumstances should we interpret the pain in our lives as a punishment for past events. Instead, pain is a specific, rough providence that comes from the Creator, pointing the right direction for attaining the thought of creation. If a person understands the pains, he or she can experience them alone, mentally, bringing them about actively rather than waiting until they push him or her from above. In this way a person advances his or her development.

But just because you may not feel any pain, does not mean that you are on the right track. Rather, you are simply in a phase where the Creator does not demand anything specific of you and doesn't push you in any specific direction. Not feeling pain is a sign that your time has not yet come.

We come to study Kabbalah when life's events bring us to it. The first phase—being persistent about learning—is not an independent decision, because at that point we are still under the influence of the preliminary push from above. But continuing to study depends on our independent efforts to be aware of what we were brought here for and on continuous efforts toward that purpose.

Each soul has a specific assignment in this world. Some come down for a certain purpose at the end of which they retire early from the world. Such was the soul of the Holy Ari, who passed away at age thirty-six, leaving behind an enormous amount of writings.

From the fall of the souls from the degree of *Adam ha Rishon* to the degree of this world, all the information about all the degrees of descent is kept within the souls. These souls robe bodies in this world and compel us to go through the entire evolutionary process from this world back to the place from which we began to fall, realizing all those *reshimot* found in them after the descent.

7

CHANGING REALITY

Can we overpower our own desire? Should we or should we not fight our own desires? After all, how can we know what is in store for us in this lifetime? That depends on our degree of spiritual development, which determines everything inside us and what we can and cannot do. The answer is to indeed fight, but just to realize that we cannot do anything by ourselves, and also to study ourselves. That is what we were given our minds for, in addition to our desires.

We attain everything within our *kelim* (vessels), our emotions. Our world consists of the overall impressions we receive from our senses, and this is how we perceive reality. If our senses change, or if we add another sense, then our world will change as well. Hence, we expand our world by changing our senses and acquiring new senses, as if rising from world to world on the ladder of worlds. By that we change the reality in which we exist.

BITTER AND SWEET, TRUE AND FALSE

In the spiritual world, things can only exist in pairs: pleasure or the absence of it, true and sweet, false and bitter. The truth is always sweet, and the lie is always bitter, and they always correspond. But that situation doesn't exist in our world. Falsehood is not bitter, and truth is not sweet. In our world we constantly face tough decisions: to choose the sweet but superficial and false way, or the bitter but sincere way.

We cannot resist the desires that surface in us. Our bodies can only distinguish between bitter and sweet, while our minds know the difference between true and false. But we can indirectly try to realize that what we consider sweet in our world is in fact bad, and then we can feel the bitter in that sweetness. Thus, the intellectual choice helps us change the choice of the body. For example, a certain man has been smoking since he was very young and enjoys it. He will quit smoking only when he is convinced of the damage it will bring him, and then smoking will become bitter for him.

That sort of entanglement was created with the sin of the first man. In the world of *Atzilut*, there was a direct link between bitter and sweet and true and false. In that world, the bitter indicated truth, altruism, bestowal, and greater closeness to the Creator. But after the sin of the first man and the breaking of his soul, sparks from the shattering descended below the world of *Atzilut* and were mixed up to such an extent that falsehood became sweet and truth became bitter.

A person climbs to spirituality via three lines: the right, the left, and the middle line. From the right line he or she receives light; from the left, desire; and in the middle line he or she builds the screen that corrects the desire. Thus, we must constantly move between the lines until we reach the world of *Atzilut*, where they unite, and the spiritual sweetness of living "for the Creator" merges with the bitterness of living only "for oneself."

THE SOCIAL IMPLICATIONS OF
KABBALAH

People who begin to study Kabbalah often feel embarrassed about their new interest. This need not be the case, and neither should their families feel uncomfortable about it, because to study Kabbalah is to study the structure of the world, the system of creation. For the time being, it is merely a theoretical practice, but in due time, they will be able to actively change the world for their own good and for the good of their families.

Therefore, this conflict within families is unnecessary. It is important to stress that our relatives needn't do anything with which they are uncomfortable, and no one should force them to adhere to any kind of tradition. The study of the wisdom of Kabbalah will render those who practice it a deeper understanding of the world around them and will enable them to choose their mode of behavior, the right type of education, and take the right steps in life, but it does not discuss any routine practice of any kind of actions, nor is its purpose to draw them to religion. The Kabbalah is about a deeper understanding of the nature of creation and the meaning of life.

No pressure should be put on those around you, but rather there should be a golden path between your behavior and that of the family. This road should comprise mutual concessions so that your family will respect what you do.

ADHESION WITH THE CREATOR

When we are attracted to someone, we are immediately filled with joy, even before we make actual contact with that person. As in corporeal love, so is the case with love for the Creator. But to prevent us from being satisfied with mere attraction, the Creator makes us feel that our situation is a low one, lacking in unity. If the Creator hadn't done that, we would be satisfied with the pleasures of desiring, without actually attaining anything. The feeling of lowness added to the desire for the Creator forces us to rise to the level of spiritual coupling and enjoy unification with the Creator.

Our sages said: "Time will do what the mind does not." And as Baal HaSulam interprets it: "Time is a sum of situations that eventuate from one another by way of cause and effect, such as days, months and years."[1] The Creator sums up and gathers together all the situations that are brought to us. God shakes us up with unpleasant incidents and situations, until there is enough torment to spark a desire for the loved one, a need to create a spiritual coupling.

That is why the soul descends from the upper world to this world and dresses in a body to incarnate in this world, so as to return to the root from which it came and cling to it again. But the soul cannot attain eternal adhesion in one cycle; it has to do it in phases. Before the soul dressed in a body, it was joined with the Creator. That adhesion has to exist despite the obstructions of the body, both corporeal and spiritual. To correct the body, we need to recognize that obstructions are not what they seem, but rather necessary catalysts to help us connect with the Creator.

It is precisely because we feel the obstructions and try to struggle with them in a heroic battle that we increase our desire for the Creator, so that we can once again be united as we were before the soul was clothed in a body, with the same power and intensity. The adhesion between us and the Creator is strengthened by the very struggles we endure in seeking out that connection.

There is always contact between us and the Creator, but for us to be able to feel His love, the Creator places an obstruction before us called the body—the desire for every pleasure possible apart from the Creator. To truly understand the Creator's love for us, we must gradually uproot the obstructions of the body, thought by thought. In other words, we must recognize the fact that each pleasure that distracts us from the desire to know the Creator is a bad one. As we struggle with each obstruction, we have a new feeling toward the loved one.

The Creator takes into account everything that is done to us, and when we have experienced the right amount of situations, when we earnestly desire for adhesion with the Creator with all our strength, nonstop, only then comes the moment of adhesion.

Only when we have reached the state of adhesion can we justify what the Creator sends us, from the lowest situations to the highest spiritual acts. Then we realize that everything that happens in life happens *because* of the Creator's love and desire to unite with us. That, in turn, creates in us a never-ending and unlimited love for the Creator.

But as long as the soul is not filled with light, the sensation of sadness increases, because the desire is not yet satisfied. Because of that the person feels torments and tortures to the same extent that he or she yearns for adhesion. In the beginning of each stage of life, we must situate ourselves correctly toward everything that happens to us. First, we must obtain the feeling that there is "me" and there is everything around "me." Then we must realize that the pressure we feel from our environment has a purpose and that the environment is an upper force that acts wisely and intentionally, with a predefined purpose and plan. The Creator knows what He does and why, but we do not. All we have to do is recognize the fact that it is all done in our favor.

The Creator and the creature strain to renew their connection. We try to see that every situation comes from the Creator; hence the Creator keeps sending new thoughts, usually in the form of obstacles. We must realize that every new thought that enters our minds is received from the Creator with the goal of attaining adhesion. We must look for the good, the eternal and perfect nature of adhesion with the Creator, from whence our souls came. Only when the soul is reunited with the Creator can it be fulfilled.

We should detect that in everything that happens there is I, the Creator, and the incident between us. Every situation is created to bring us into contact with Him. At first, they are only thoughts. But afterward, they become feelings and sensations. In the end, we will find that the entire body, meaning all the desires, the thoughts, the entire spiritual and corporeal systems, and all the worlds will no longer be concealed. They will no longer be screens and obstacles between humanity and the Creator. You will feel that the obstructions, concealments, and the entire system of the body will become an inner system for you and will intensify your connection with the Creator. After all, the purpose of the body is unification, not separation. Know that all the worlds are inside you, though at the moment you only feel them externally, as a result of the corruption of our vessels.

The innermost part of the *partzuf* (the soul) is the root, called "the root of the soul." Then there are outer layers, which are called (from inside out): *neshama* (soul); *guf* (body); *levush* (dressing/clothing); *heichal* (temple, palace); or *Adam, levush, bait, hatzer, midbar* (Adam, dressing, house, yard, and desert, respectively). Thus we see that spiritual attainment is always attained gradually. Our current image of reality is a consequence of the second restriction, where a part of the vessels, the desires of the soul, went out of order—meaning they stopped being inner vessels and became external ones, which are forbidden for use.

These external vessels—*bait, hatzer,* and *midbar*—create the sensation of an outer world in us. Everything we perceive as external will become internal at the end of correction, when these desires are corrected and the world as we know it will vanish. Baal HaSulam writes that all the worlds exist inside us.[2] At the end of correction, the whole world will "enter" us; the substance of the world will become inner substance, over which we will feel the presence of the Creator.

The most important thing is to maintain contact with the Creator at all times and in all places, even in the lowest degree. Baal HaSulam also writes that the greatest punishment for a person is the detachment from the thought of the Creator, even for a moment, because that disconnects one from the source of life.

The connection with the Creator can only be strengthened through obstructions, because when a person feels good he or she becomes addicted to that feeling and forgets to think about the origin of the feeling. But when one feels bad, one immediately begins to search for the source of the bad to abolish it.

At first, the Creator purposely sends us sensations of fear, insecurity, shortage, and lack. But this is just the first part of the process—the coercion. We approach the Creator only to overcome those negative feelings. But after some time we begin to want the Creator independently until we cannot sleep for the lovesickness. This is a state of corporeal-egoistic love, and is precisely the situation we should come to; the state is called *Lo Lishma* (not for Her name).

We advance in such a way that this entire stage of *Lo Lishma* (time of preparation), below the barrier and right before we attain spirituality, is essential to increase the desires, the vessels of selfish desire for the Creator. Only then comes the opposite operation, the passage from *Lo Lishma* to *Lishma* (for Her name), from egoism to altruism, from the will to receive to the will to give.

CHANGING REALITY THROUGH INNER WORK

Reality changes because if we strengthen our contact with the Creator, there will no longer be a need for pain, the very same pains that are initiated from above to bring about that contact.

Thus, the external circumstances will change, since we will no longer require the same pains.

For some, the individual is squeezed to the bone by the Creator to obtain his or her connection. But for others, the Creator acts differently, settling for slowly and egoistically turning them toward Him. It might be described in the following way: the individual is at the top of the pyramid and the majority is at the bottom of it, and because of that he or she is treated differently. Also, the individual develops the aim, while the masses join their collective desire to that individual. That is why their work is so different, though they are both a part of the thought of creation.

People do not understand why changes in the world occur or how. But the torments they suffer make them search subconsciously for an upper power and pray to it because there is no one else on whom to rely. That prayer, that earthy still prayer, works. Using the torments, the Creator puts us in a no-win situation and corners us until we actually start looking for an alternative planet to live on. But that planet cannot be found, except in the Creator.

For example, it is interesting to consider why the Creator brought the Jewish people to the corporeal land of Israel, rather then to the spiritual one. The return to Israel was the result of a prayer that was lying in our subconscious and of the pain and suffering we Jews had endured over many years. We prayed for our own place, and we received that place. But if we had truly understood that our sufferings had happened for a certain purpose, then our prayer, the prayer of the unsatisfied mass, would have been aimed differently, and a new solution would have arisen on a different level, a spiritual one.

Killing, disease, and torment are such a substantial part of our lives because of the law that says that everything must return to its root. These obstructions were formed during the detachment of the soul from its root. They are rungs it climbed down on, making it more and more coarse and egoistic. Hence, neutralizing these obstructions, these attributes, can be done by bringing the soul back to its root. And there is only one way to neutralize this egoism: by recognizing death, sickness, and unhappiness as obstructions. Once we achieve this realization, we can begin to draw ourselves toward the center of the world and reconnect with our root.

This is the law of equivalence of form, which we have discussed earlier. Like a piece of metal in a magnetic field, the soul is naturally drawn to its ultimate degree of adhesion with the Creator. Every state of being other than complete cohesion is transitory, leading us in the same direction. Whether we are conscious of it or not, we are being led back to that original state. But when we are aware of the process, and we see things as they really are, the process is sped up.

It is not that we should aspire to perform only this law of equivalence of form, for we cannot change our inner traits, but we should only want to change things inside us in accordance with that law. We should want that law to exist even if we had the power to cancel it.

The way to adopt higher qualities, ones that we still do not possess, is always according to the principle of "above reason," meaning above the mind. There is no example of this in our world, because we cannot attain the mind of the Creator, the upper mind. All we can do is develop the mind we already have. But in the spiritual world there is a switch: the human mind is replaced with that of the Creator. It is a slow and gradual process. In each degree, a person gets an additional portion of the mind of the Creator to use instead of his or her own. That is why in every stage, a person should work toward erasing his or her own mind and replacing it with the mind of the Creator. To help us, the Creator sends us an image of the world that we cannot understand with our mind; we cannot accept or justify it and see it as a picture that comes from the Creator to benefit us.

In other words, the discrepancy between that image and the current image of the world we see in our minds lets us understand that events unfold according to the mind of the Creator and not our own. Thus, people realize that they have no choice but to change their minds, so that they can agree with the picture of the world that spreads before them.

A person who progresses this way is called "righteous" because his or her means of advancement is to self-correct in such a way that he or she can justify every situation in favor of the Creator. A righteous person is one who thinks that the Creator is right. If an individual is aware of the fact that when feeling dissatisfaction with life, he or she is in fact cursing the Creator, then that dissatisfaction with life is tantamount to dissatisfaction with the origin of life. It hurts this person to curse the Creator, and so he or she asks for one thing only: the power to justify the Creator in every situation.

CORRECTING MYSELF, CORRECTING THE WORLD

Our sensors are very unrefined. We cannot feel much of what happens inside our own bodies, such as molecular collisions or the birth of new cells. Therefore, there are many changes that need to take place for us to start feeling anything. Before any feeling is created in us, millions of wheels must revolve inside, entire mechanisms have to perform many corrections before those corrections are felt by us.

The study of the Kabbalah works on various levels of our soul, in attributes of the will to receive that we cannot feel just yet. A person reads but understands nothing, and so feels no reason to continue to study. The person feels this way because the text is working on attributes below the threshold of his or her feelings. It is like a person filling a glass of water and wondering why the bottom part of the glass has to be filled first before he or she can drink off the top. There seems to be no reason to be concerned with the other parts.

Our will to receive is corrected through the study of the Kabbalah. The study deals with the different levels of the soul, the vessel and the desire, which are at the bottom of the glass. We don't touch them, do not drink them, and do not feel their actual taste until they reach the top, where we actually begin to feel them.

But very slowly one does begin to feel. It is a slow process because the will to receive, our egoism, is very deep and complex. Slowly we adapt to the light, the number of attributes in the will to receive matches that of the light. Therefore, even if we don't understand what we are studying, we must continue to study with the intention of attaining the attributes of the light, and not for the purpose of mere understanding.

Without this intention, without the desire to attain the light, nothing will be gained. The power of the study and the light works on us according to our power of intent and desire. The disclosure is a slow and gradual process, but if we connect everything we feel with the primary question, "What is the meaning of my life?" all other questions, which are consequences of this one, are answered by themselves.

When a person corrects his or her desire and aim, all other parts of creation below—animal, vegetative, and inanimate—participate in the ascent, though they are unaware of it. They cannot feel it, because it is something that can only be felt in the human degree, in spiritual changes. But the general effect of the light is felt at all levels of creation.

The other parts of creation do not question the meaning of their lives, but the fact that humans do and can study the right, genuine Kabbalah books with the intent to connect themselves with the light joins all other parts of creation to their question, including and correcting them within. This is why we can feel nature inside us. For example, when we fly over mountains, their mighty silence and intense expectation for the revelation of the Creator can be felt clearly.

We raise all parts of nature with us. Because we are the only beings with the goal to give as well as receive and because we can ask ourselves the essential question "What am I living for?" we are the source of correction for the whole world, and the only ones obliged to perform it. The world is changing according to us: if we change a little for the better, so does the world. Those changes are so small that we cannot detect them, yet they do necessarily and immediately happen, both for better and for worse. Creation is always under a gradual process of development (evolution), which depends on the changes of humanity.

Power is an external manifestation of a desire. When I want something, I insist, I push and pull, I do anything I can to get what I want. When we speak of the powers of nature, such as gravity, electromagnetic energy, or chemical bonds, in the end, they are all essentially two: the pulling force, which wants to receive, and the pushing force, which wants to give. They are the only two forces in nature, and everything else is but combinations of them.

In the spiritual world there is only the creature and the Creator. The creature is the desire to give to the Creator, and the Creator is the desire to give to the creature. All other creations have no freedom of choice and are therefore called "angels." Our work is to collect those desires to receive, or angels, that do not have freedom of choice and add them to ones that do have that freedom to correct those desires.

At this point we should ask the following question: If willpower is that strong, then why can't Kabbalists, being the ones who perform all the corrections of nature, manage all of nature? The answer is that they can indeed. A Kabbalist is a person who has corrected his or her nature and attained the higher degrees of creation, a person who can see how the world is managed and by which laws it abides. Kabbalists agree with these laws because they have corrected themselves and sustain the existence of these laws with the power of will. That is what gives Kabbalists the permission to manage nature.

RISING ABOVE THIS WORLD

All parts of creation, ourselves included, are sustained and managed by a force called nature, or Creator, whose attribute is bestowal (in Hebrew the word is *hashpaa,* which comes from the root word *shefa,* bounty). When a Kabbalist attains a certain degree of correction and has acquired a certain amount of will to bestow, meaning to give, he or she can join in the management of nature. Being in the degree of speaking, the Kabbalist can be included in the degrees of still, vegetative, and animate, according to his or her degree, add much bounty and change the laws of nature. Through the Kabbalist, nature becomes more merciful.

Depending on how corrected he or she is compared to them, a Kabbalist can raise other souls as well. The amount of influence a Kabbalist has on others depends on the degree of his or her soul and its uniqueness, meaning what part of the soul of the first man it comes from—*rosh* (head), *guf* (body), *raglaim* (legs), or some other part. The Kabbalist's degree of correction greatly influences the rising of the souls and their readiness for correction. This is one way the Kabbalists help the world.

The stronger the illumination of the upper light, the more one is able to discern right from wrong. Just as when one walks using the light of a flashlight and can see only as far as the light reaches, so our egoism determines how well we can tell right from wrong. In other words, seeing our true nature, how evil we are, and feeling a need to correct those things only happens in proportion to the degree the Creator is revealed to us. Therefore, if we ask of the Creator to reveal Himself to us so that we can see ourselves for what we are and correct ourselves, and not for egoistic pleasure, then that is the prayer He answers.

The problem is that we don't acknowledge that the Creator will not listen to our cry because the torments have a reason! The Creator wants us to attain correction through these plagues. We have to understand that and reply: "You are doing right in causing me difficulty. Because of that I see the evil in me. However, give me a chance to see how I can correct myself." That is precisely the kind of prayer that the Creator is waiting for, and that is what we should ask for. Our pleas should be directed toward correction. We need to study Kabbalah to come to this realization.

There is only one desire in the world: to delight the creatures. There is only one goal: to make the creatures feel eternal pleasure. The unique thought of the Creator is the one thing that exists in the world; it is everything and everything works toward it. Hence, everything abides by one law only—to return creation to the Creator, to the light, to pleasure.

When you ask for pleasures for yourself, you must realize that that can only be obtained through correction. Therefore, instead of asking the Creator for favors, we should ask for correction. Through that correction, we will obtain pleasure. One who realizes that suffering comes to inspire correction has already begun the correction itself. We gradually attain wisdom and change ourselves as a result. We learn not to relate to the suffering itself, but to look at who is sending us that suffering and why. We should feel the pains as a means without which we would not respond and turn to the Creator.

We must rise above bad feelings and start to use our mind. Start by examining why you feel so badly and why you are being beaten down by life. Surely there is a higher force that sends you these troubles. Ask yourself what its purpose is. At that point, you may begin to feel anger: "Is this what You call 'desire to delight your creatures'? There is nothing worse than what You are sending me!" When a person begins to ask these questions, he or she immediately goes beyond the suffering itself, realizing that there is a reason for the trouble. From that point on, the person begins to correct him- or herself and thus improve his or her situation.

A NEW CONSCIOUSNESS

In order for the world to change, there has to be a new consciousness among the public, one that is above emotions. There has to be reason as well as emotion in the way we relate to the world. We need reason to relate to good and bad critically and to realize that if we feel bad, it must mean that there is a reason and a purpose for it. The public is stuck in a cycle of merely "feeling bad," or "feeling good." It can take hundreds of years before people start asking: "Why is this happening to me?"

Our goal is to explain where our present state is leading us. As Baal HaSulam wrote,[3] "Religion is not for the good of the people, but for the good of the worker," meaning that the purpose of religion is not to benefit people, or to benefit the Creator, but to benefit those who are working to be corrected. The entire world was created for that ultimate goal. But if you judge what happens to you only by feelings of "good" or "bad," you remain in the degrees of still, vegetative, or animate and never advance to the degree of speaking, the degree we need to complete our correction.

The Creator does not forget us. Every day more and more pains are added to our world. Our only problem is how much we will have to suffer before we realize that torments come for the sole purpose of awakening in us something above the sensation of pain. People think there is nothing they can do, and that this is the price we pay for living in this world. But that attitude is nothing more than an escape from recognizing the reason for the pains. Instead of asking why this happens to us, and perhaps acknowledging that there is a purpose to it, we calm ourselves down and accept it. We try to reduce the painful sensation. People die every day and we still find a way to make ourselves comfortable with it. That is what happens in our society today. Acting in such a way is like being an ostrich that hides its head in the sand in the face of danger. Such actions have become a strategy in our world. Politicians brag about their narrow-mindedness and their lack of understanding in what we face.

The person who concerns him- or herself with the reason for the pains in the world is different from others in that he or she has a more developed soul. Therefore, it is that person's duty to explain to others that there is a reason for the pains— namely, that they demand of us to unite with the upper force. We need only recognize that the pain is actually the Creator bringing us closer to the good. If we begin to think about the goal, instead of our pain and egoism, we will begin to solve all our problems.

HUMANKIND AS A SPIRITUAL DEGREE

As soon as a spark of spirituality appears in you, even as an impulse that is still hidden from your eyes, you stop being satisfied with your life. You begin to search for something beyond money, honor, sex, food, power, and knowledge and don't know where to find what you really want. This is the first time you feel that there is something beyond your surroundings in this world. That spark evolves later on to become the desire for contact and adhesion with the Creator.

All throughout this journey, a person is defined by his or her unique desire to cleave to the Creator, differentiating humanity from other life forms. People still have within them the desires of the still, vegetative, and animate degrees, but our specific degree is measured by the intensity of our desire for the Creator.

In his introduction to the book *Panim Meirot Umasbirot (Illuminating and Welcoming Face)*, Baal HaSulam writes that all the desires except the one called "human" are measured by the desired object:

- In the *still degree*, desires are turned toward food, sex, and family, meaning bodily and beastly pleasures.

- In the *vegetative degree*, desires are turned toward money and security.

- In the *animate degree*, desires are turned toward power, control, and respect.

- In the *speaking degree*, desires are turned toward spirituality. A person's desires have by now evolved to such an extent that he or she desires something outside the physical world.

Everyone has some attributes that they want to keep as they are, and ones that they want to exchange for spirituality. To the extent that one is willing to give up one's inner attributes for the purpose of attaining spirituality, one is called "human," and to the extent that one is unable to give up certain attributes, one is called "beast."

The beastly degree is one where a person does not want to change, meaning refuses to change inner traits. For example, a person may think that, for the time being, he or she is unable to get rid of certain inner traits, even for the spiritual goal. Until that person is able to give up something, he or she is called a "beast." That, in fact, is the contradiction between the general populace and the Kabbalist. This distinction represents the greatest distinction of all—the difference between ourselves and the Creator. The general populace advances according to its nature, whereas the unique individual, the Kabbalist, who yearns for connection with the Creator, advances according to the attributes of the Creator, which already exist within him or her.

The main difference between the Kabbalists and other people is in the education they do or do not receive. For the general society it is best to stay conservative, in a still degree, unchanging. Everything that is taught in society should be kept without change. That way, people keep themselves safe from confusion and assimilation. However, for the individual, the more different and disobedient his or her personality is to others, guided only by the feelings in his or her heart, the nobler it is. Therefore, the situations faced by the unique individual should not be mixed with those of the ordinary person, who is one of many. One who feels a desire for the Creator must develop his or her uniqueness through the study of the Kabbalah.

A NEW ERA

The study of Kabbalah was forbidden to the masses for many generations. Kabbalists prohibited the study to women, children, and men under forty (in Kabbalah, age forty signifies intelligence—*bina*—when a person already understands that the purpose of life is giving, something the public cannot understand because they are still at a beastly level). In other words, this kind of learning was forbidden to those who hadn't evolved enough to be able to study Kabbalah.

However, as soon as there is a spark, a sensation of the appearance of a soul, one *must* study Kabbalah. When Rav Kook was asked, "Who can study Kabbalah?" he replied simply, "Anyone who wants to!" Desire is the one and only requirement for the development of the soul.

Baal HaSulam writes that if a person is ready to study Kabbalah, but refrains from doing so, then that person is the reason for all the disasters because he or she did not contribute his or her share to the management of creation. The collective law of reality is built in such a way that if a person must take an active part in the leadership of reality and refrains from doing so, the rough part of nature comes in its place. That switch between the force of humanity and the force of nature is felt in our world as tragedies and pains. As soon as we begin to feel a desire for the Creator, we must learn how to correct ourselves and thus change reality. If we refrain from doing that, we bring about more evil in the world.

My teacher, Rav Baruch Ashlag, said that before the time of Baal HaSulam (1884–1954), all the books about Judaism were written by Kabbalists who wrote from their personal levels of spiritual attainment. Throughout history, Kabbalists were the ones to define the edification of the nation. For example, during the British mandate in Israel (1917–1948), Baal HaSulam tried to publish a Kabbalistic magazine. He saw that the time had come when the public wanted to approach the spiritual degree that only a chosen few had reached before. Hence, he tried to explain to the people about the Kabbalah. But there was still a need to convey it in a simple and easily understandable manner. Only then would everyone be able to make their own choices, and the ones who were really attracted to the Upper One would continue to study.

Why is this edification needed now, while it was not needed a hundred or two hundred years ago? Only after the Holocaust, and the return to the land of Israel, did a new era begin in the evolution of the souls. When the Creator brought us back to the land of Israel, He also brought us back to the spiritual soil, giving us an opportunity for spiritual operations and sublime attainments. That process is only just beginning; hence the new need to explain Kabbalah to the entire generation today.

In the past there wasn't a need to study Kabbalah. Baal HaSulam wrote that there were many people who attained high spiritual degrees through the written and oral Torah alone. But Kabbalah books contain a greater illumination of upper light, which can assist one in the correction process. Though all holy books were written from the highest spiritual degree of the "end of correction," the Kabbalah books that were written for our generation have a unique shine to them, instead of a general illumination, because they were written especially for those who want spiritual elevation in our time.

Although a person can reach such a high degree of understanding that he or she can no longer make mistakes, in the beginning and middle of the path toward such understanding, there are many different routes, according to the root of his or her soul. Therefore, Kabbalists were not always open with one another, and sometimes concealed themselves even from fellow Kabbalists.

Once, when my teacher finished a discussion with a certain person, I asked him if that person was a Kabbalist. He replied, "I think he is, partly." I asked him, surprised, "What do you mean 'partly'?" He answered, "He does not want to show himself, so it is impossible to see. He must show you his screen. If a Kabbalist does not want to be exposed, he can appear before you as a drunk, or a worthless person. But if he does wish to expose himself, he displays his screen, and you begin to work together with a collective vessel, and then everything changes. It is like two experts doing something they are completely preoccupied with. They understand one another perfectly; they don't even need words; they share a common revelation."

There are many ways to achieve correction, and one does not contradict the other. Souls stay apart because the unification between them happens only in the degree of the end of correction. The greatest differences are then corrected and sorted out, right before the last and greatest unification with the upper light. The greatest observations are still to come. We must understand that this is a natural process that the collective soul, meaning the whole of humankind, experiences. The general society should remain as it is, but the worthy individuals, and there are quite a few of those, should not be denied the study of Kabbalah.

Kabbalists do not say that we must teach everyone, but in our time in history it must be understood that Kabbalah is a method of development that obligates everyone. People often come, listen, and leave, and by doing so they prepare themselves for the next stage in the correction. Reading the books of Kabbalah is also a correction, and the rest is up to the Creator.

Something learned is never lost. If one comes to Kabbalah and then leaves, that person will return, even if it is two or three hundred years later. Each person is built differently. There is no wrong or right, but only a certain order. There is no way to resist what is decided above. We must do as Baal HaSulam instructed, spreading his books, which were written especially for our generation, and circulating the knowledge in them. Whomever catches onto this knowledge needs it.

It is always better to be either on the side of the careless, beastly nature or in constant contact with the Creator as "human," than to be left hanging in the middle. Today, however, most of us are stuck in the middle, which is why we cannot enjoy our lives. It was once enough for us to enjoy a sports match on television, go for a walk, or spend time in a bar. But we are now in a transition period between human and beast, and hence we feel bad. This unpleasant time can go on for many years; there is nowhere to run from it. As King David says, "If I ascend up into heaven, Thou art there; if I make my bed in the nether-world, behold, Thou art there" (Ps. 139:8).

A person who compares him- or herself to the Creator feels that he or she is corrupted and needs correction. The perfection only appears to someone after seeing his or her inherent evil. Someone brought up by a different spiritual method for perfection cannot feel that something is missing. But one day that person, too, will begin to feel the point in the heart and, inside it, the Creator. Then he or she, too, will feel the difference and will come to the recognition of evil.

Thus, Kabbalah must not be circulated aggressively or coercively so as not to interfere with each individual's development. We should ask ourselves what we were born for, what the meaning of our lives is. All we need to do is bring ourselves to ask these questions.

Human beings are the only ones who can detach themselves from the reward. It does not mean that they are not rewarded, but they receive a different kind of payment. First they restrict themselves, so as not to receive anything for themselves. This is called "crossing the barrier." After that an entirely different kind of calculation takes over—a calculation in favor of the Creator, in which giving to the Creator is the goal and the purpose. All calculations from then on are performed to detect the goal as precisely as possible: What is the goal, what is the aim, and what do we strive to attain through all these efforts? The conclusion we arrive at is that we want to give to the Creator as much as possible.

There is a Creator, and there is a creature. The creature goes through various phases, from the dawn of human history until today and until the end of correction. We live and relive in this world many times over. We evolve from one life to the next, and there is a purpose to that. Starting from a certain degree, a person becomes active in his or her own evolution. At this stage we feel a calling from above, as though something is pulling, pushing us toward something.

If a person knows that these things actually exist, he or she will speed up his or her own development. The minute he or she learns about it, a person begins to read about it and accumulate knowledge. That awakens the shine of the surrounding light, and his or her development is accelerated.

A MATURE APPROACH TO PAIN

When I read the newspapers and listen to the radio, I see that the nations of the world treat me differently because I belong to the Jewish people. The attitude is laden with hostile, anti-Semitic emotions.

Even within Israel and around it there are peoples who wish to destroy, or at the very least, subdue the Jewish people. Our challenge is to treat this situation as one that comes to us from the Creator and that it is happening in our favor, so that we will change our line of thinking and the way we work. It is happening so that we will rise above our normal human reaction, from an instinctive reaction to what our eyes see to questioning the reasons for what is happening around us.

If I do not relate to the phenomenon of anti-Semitism as it is, but to the reason behind it, I will then be operating in the spiritual degree called "humanity." This is the only way for me to develop an ability to understand the essence of events. Instead of running away from situations, like an animal runs from a hunter, I can actually change external causes.

As I have said throughout this book, there is only one reason for all the pains of this world: to make us wonder at their meaning, to raise us from a level of aimlessly suffering to a level where we think about and analyze the reason and the purpose for the pains. The spreading of the wisdom of Kabbalah brings the purpose and cause of the pains to the public awareness. By doing so, we can shorten the amount of time it takes for every person to understand the cause for suffering and realize that there is no pain without a reason, that it comes from the Creator. The purpose of the operations that the Creator performs on us is to develop in us, through a series of negative situations, a grown-up attitude toward pain. Therefore, we should not escape them, only use them and see them as a gift from the Creator.

If we use them correctly, we can turn them into a vessel that will be constantly filled with infinite knowledge and delight. If we rise above the ordinary feeling of suffering and try to understand what causes it, then instead of feeling the stick, we would feel the Creator, the giver of the pain, the one who holds the stick. That is what the Creator wants from us! And then the pain will stop! The Creator is leading us to this goal, through our own egoistic desires to delight ourselves alone. Just like a child is tempted with sweets, the Creator sends us ascents (good feelings) and descents (bad feelings) and gradually leads us to want to be in permanent connection with Him, to need Him.

In the beginning, this connection between ourselves and the Creator is based on our benefit—we want the sweets as a child does. But later on, because there is a need to survive, we develop that connection and begin an entirely different phase of development, a completely different attitude to pleasure and reward. From a will to receive pleasure only through the body, we move on to a desire to receive pleasure above the body, a reward that does not depend on the sensations of the body.

In other words, we begin to understand that there can be a much higher reward than the bodily one. The reward that we expect no longer comes from the fear that once compelled us to maintain contact with the Creator. We feel as though the fears of the body slowly disappear like a long coat slipping off our shoulders, or like a snake sloughing its skin. We no longer act by the calculation of what will be good or bad for us.

No longer reliant on this life to maintain contact with the Creator, a new need forms in us: to be in constant connection with the Creator, freed from the physical body and its feelings. That need creates in us a permanent desire to feel the Creator. It becomes so strong that it pains us if bodily pleasures distract our mind from contact with the Creator.

If a person experiences this entire chain of feelings and insights, he or she begins to thank the Creator and love Him for having sent all these "negative" experiences, which actually brought him or her to contact the Creator. Therefore, it is most important to strengthen this feeling so that no corporeal obstruction can break the inner connection with the Creator, but rather intensify it.

When this contact is attained, it takes the form of worlds (degrees of contact with the Creator, described here from the least to the greatest): the worlds of *Assiya, Yetzira, Beria, Atzilut,* and *Ein Sof.* When that contact intensifies, it is called an ascent in the spiritual worlds. In the end, there is such a strong connection that we attach ourselves completely to the Creator and unite with Him.

Kabbalists who are in contact with the Creator, while still being in their physical bodies, feel their mission, in addition to their sensation of the Creator. Their mission is to help all those who live in a corporeal body to attain contact with the Creator, if only a little bit.

NOTES

Chapter 3

1. *Adam Kadmon* (the first man) is the root world, the world from which all other spiritual worlds emerge.

2. The name *Atzilut* (Emanation) comes from the word *Etzlo* (at His place). This is the world where the complete unity with the Creator is first obtained, and where the guidance system of reality is found.

3. In the world of *Beria* (Creation) one completes one's personal correction. It is also the intermediary degree between *Atzilut* and the lower worlds.

4. In the world of *Yetzira* (Formation) one begins one's actual correction. Here the guidance of the Creator is divided into good and bad.

5. *Assiya* (Action) is the first spiritual world, where one is completely passive and merely observes the work of the Creator. In that state, one's attributes are still corrupted. Thus, the name pertains not to the creature's actions, but to the Creator's.

Chapter 4

1. Major scholars from a variety of disciplines express themselves regarding the crisis that their fields of knowledge might be, or are already, experiencing. Some of them can be found in John Horgan's *The End of Science* (New York: Broadway Books, 1996), pp. 46, 58, 176, 178.

2. According to the World Health Organization (WHO), depression was the fourth most common cause of illness in the world (approximately 121 million people) and will soar to the second most common by the year 2020. These figures also indicate that depression is one of the key factors of suicide. Over a million people die of suicide every year, and between ten and twenty million people attempt suicide the world over. For more details, see World Health Organization, *Mental Health, Suicide Rates per 100,000 by Country, Year and Sex.*

3. According to the White House Office of National Drug Control Policy (ONDCP), *Drug Data Summary,* March 2003, psychoactive drugs are being increasingly used all over the world. In the United States, for example, 42 percent of the population use drugs.

4. Y. L. Ashlag, "Introduction to the Tree of Life," in *Sefer HaHakdamot,* trans. Chaim Ratz (Israel: 1976), item 3.

5. Ashlag, "Introduction to the Tree of Life," item 3.

6. "All the damages come to a man through the self reception that is imprinted in him." Y. L. Ashlag, "The Essence of Religion and Its Purpose," in *Matan Torah,* trans. Chaim Ratz (Jerusalem, Israel: Ohr HaGanuz, 1995).

7. Y. L. Ashlag, "The Peace," in *Matan Torah,* trans. Chaim Ratz (Jerusalem, Israel: Ohr HaGanuz, 1995).

8. Y. L. Ashlag, "The Freedom," in *Matan Torah,* trans. Chaim Ratz (Jerusalem, Israel: Ohr HaGanuz, 1995).

9. See notes number 2 and number 3 above.

10. Y. L. Ashlag, "A Speech for the Completion of the Zohar," in *Matan Torah,* trans. Chaim Ratz (Jerusalem, Israel: Ohr HaGanuz, 1995).

11. Ashlag, "A Speech for the Completion of the Zohar."

Chapter 7

1. Y. L. Ashlag, *Talmud Eser Sefirot,* trans. Chaim Ratz (Jerusalem, Israel: M. Klar, 1956), part 1, Questions and Answers, Answer 16.

2. Y. L. Ashlag, "Introduction to the Preface to the Wisdom of Kabbalah," in *Sefer HaHakdamot,* trans. Chaim Ratz (Israel: 1976), item 1.

3. Ashlag, "The Essence of Religion and Its Purpose."